FINDING COURAGE

*A Single Mother's Story of Heartbreak,
Redemption, and Dating*

DORY DANIEL

PAGE PUBLISHING, INC.
Conneaut Lake, PA

First originally published by Page Publishing 2021

ISBN 978-1-6624-5295-6 (pbk)
ISBN 978-1-6624-5296-3 (digital)

Printed in the United States of America

Have you ever felt like you are destined for pain and suffering through a sad and lonely life with a constant broken heart? Or maybe, you are tired of picking up the pieces of your destroyed self again and again? Well, you are not alone. This book is about my journey of love, loss, self-discovery, and redemption. It is about my fall from the ecstasies of true love to the bottom of the deep, dark, lonely canyon. It is about how I struggled to climb out time after time, only to find myself falling again. This book is also about my discovery of self and how I am learning to take action in order to prevent myself from being lost and lonely. I hope this book speaks to you and gives you some refuge, some gems of hope, or whatever it is you are looking for. At the very least, maybe this book will bring you some laughter at the crazy situations life and love can bring.

PART 1

CHAPTER 1

Yes, I'm single, and you'll have to be
fucking amazing to change that.

—Anonymous

Let's start with my dating life. Well, currently it is nonexistent, but that is by choice, well, kind of. Some other factors for my lackluster love life are this crazy global pandemic thingy, the fact that I am raising two teenage boys on my own, and having just been left by what I thought was the love of my life. So yeah, I would like to say it is by choice, but some of you and, let's be honest, parts of me, may disagree. But, regardless of the reasons, this is my current situation. However, I am not satisfied with that fact, so now I am on a quest to make a real change. I am ready to grab this life of mine by my talons. I am ready to live the life I want. I am ready for my dreams to be realized. This is my quest to redeem myself from my self-pity, and to save my love life from total extinction. This quest is absolutely crucial if I want to be happy. So if any of you want to join me in this quest, then you better be ready to dig through the muck of our failed relationships and prepare yourself for vulnerable awareness and immediate action.

All journeys must have a place to start, a trailhead, if you will. Where does your journey start? Were you doomed from conception? Were you raised for a life of beauty, but somewhere, somehow, you ended up in the dumpster? How do our formative years affect our current situation? I have thought about this a lot, and I think that for me, my childhood experiences and lessons are the foundation on which I stand. And, if this foundation is strong (which I believe it is), then how did I end up in crumbles? To answer that question, I must go back, start at the beginning, my childhood.

My family life was typical for that of a middle-class white American family. My parents raised my sister and me in an affluent mountain town in Colorado. My mother was a nurse and my father owned a retail store. They both were well educated and from wholesome families. My mother had nine siblings and my father had two. My parents both believed that the most important qualities in life were education and, above all, education. According to my parents, there was no success in life unless you had a college degree. In addition to their strict requirements of academic achievements, they also instituted a family focus on hard work, healthy diets, and an athletic lifestyle. These values were cultivated by spending time with family, being active in nature, traveling, and participating in the arts such as ballet, opera, art museums, and such. Our weekends were usually spent up at the family lake house owned by my mother's family. It was here that we would exhaust ourselves playing with our cousins, swimming in the cold-ass mountain lake, walking to town, learning to water-ski, splitting wood for the winter, building forts in the forest, and cooking and cleaning for all the guests. These activities provided my sister and me a solid foundation in the importance and pleasure of working and playing hard as a family.

During the school year, our weekdays were focused on homework, extracurricular activities, and chores. My sister and I were expected to participate in a sport and an art throughout the school year. I played volleyball and played the piano. My sister also played volleyball and was in art classes. Watching TV was reserved for Friday nights as a family. Spending time with friends was allowed on Saturdays unless we were up at the lake cabin.

To this day, my parents are still together, working their bodies to the bone and only watching TV on Friday nights. Talk about commitment!

A decent assumption one could make from the description of my childhood would be that I would have a solid education, career, and family. Well, sorry to disappoint, but somewhere I took a detour (my sister as well, but this book is not about her, sorry, dear sister).

I did succeed in the education and career department. I have two masters and I am a successful teacher. My family, well, that is different. I have been divorced for over twelve years, and I have been in and out of several serious relationships since my divorce. I am a single mother of two teenage boys, and I drive a beat-up Subaru on its last breath. I do own a home, but that is because my parents let me build a modular on their property. This modular happens to be a log cabin kit, and it is absolutely beautiful, but the only reason I was able to do this is because my mother helped me with the cost of the infrastructure and, of course, the land.

Had I stayed in my marriage, I probably would still be living in a perfect little house, with the perfect little family, with two incomes to have the perfect pastimes. But what I would lack is far more important. What I would lack is love and happiness. My parents did not really talk about being happy. Instead they focused on the importance of being responsible, polite, and fulfilling your duties. Therefore, when I decided that my happiness was suffering and that I needed to get out of my marriage, they had a really hard time understanding and accepting my decision.

Was this a generational thing? Were my parents just performing in the way that they were taught? Fulfilling their duty as parents while ignoring their own happiness? When did these ideals change? And has the pendulum swung too far the other way? How do we go about fulfilling our duties and being responsible while living the life we want and being authentic to ourselves by choosing happiness? How do we find partners and create relationships that make us happy and are not just following the rat race rulebook?

After spending time thinking about and analyzing my childhood, I have come to realize that I was never taught to choose happiness. I was taught to do my best in school, get a career, and help other people along the way. I was taught that love is a commitment and more about responsibilities than happiness. My mother always said that other people's happiness should come first and that we should always help others before we help ourselves. With a moral compass like that, it is no wonder why I have chosen the men that I have. I chose the wounded birds, the ones I knew needed my help. I chose their happiness over mine.

That brings us to the fun part, my relationships. Watch out, because these are sometimes so crazy that they are hard to believe.

I am just going to give a quick summary of the big relationships because I am going to go in-depth with each of them later as each taught me very valuable lessons and they are the reason that I am here writing this book.

Let's begin with my high school boyfriend Carter. Well, to put it simply, Carter was a dork and I was a dork. We were a match made in heaven and fell hard for each other. We stayed together for four years and then split when I went to college. Next, ex-husband Blake, according to his friends, he was a "really cool guy." This was true, he was very cool, but he was also a really big jerk! He was conceited and had a very tough exterior, and we had nothing in common. Later I found that inside this rough and tough exterior, he actually had a hurt heart. He hid it well, but I thought that I was the one that could help heal his heart. He really loved me for that, and I think that I was the only one who truly knew who he was, so when he asked me to marry him, I was flattered, and since I did not want to hurt him, I said yes. We married, had two kids, and played family for a while. But eventually, the love and companionship that I never truly had with him started to bloom elsewhere. We separated, got a divorce, and both of us moved on. The few relationships after my divorce were simply lust and distractions. Then I met Paul. We were doomed from the start. I mean, anyone who saw us together would either stare or giggle or both! He was short and I was tall. And I mean he was really short, five feet three, and I was really tall, six feet. The only possible way for me to be attracted to a man that short was if I met him first without being in his physical presence. Or in other words, the Internet. He was funny and kind, had two young kids the same age as mine. It was a seven-year relationship, two years on, two years off, and three years on. After him, I fell in love with what I thought was my soul mate, Ben. Ben and I had known each other for seven years, because he was Paul's best friend. He had red flags all over the place, but my heart was so taken that I did not pay attention to the warning signs. We moved in together, he embraced my kids like his own, I did the same with his, but that really bright huge red flag finally took center stage and he left me. That was eight months ago, and now this is where I am. My ex-husband (my children's father) moved out of state to take care of his ailing mother, so my boys, sixteen and fourteen, live with me full-time.

So yeah, you could say that I am a train wreck, or possibly a relationship nightmare. But maybe, and possibly more likely, you can relate to this recipe of disaster. Whatever it is you are thinking, just remember that we all have our issues and everyone has a struggle. This is my struggle. But in all reality, it is not a struggle, it is my past. I am no longer present in those relationships, and they have done nothing but made me who I am today. Me, whom I *love*.

But how did I get to a place of loving myself even though my life has felt very messy? Well, it is through all of those relationships that I have found some amazing lessons that have helped me learn to love and accept myself. This is my story of how I found compassion and empathy for others and, through that, strength. The strength I needed to be able to overcome the pain, heartbreak, and depression. This is my story of how I found my worth and discovered passion and desire to finally get what I want and what I deserve in *my* life.

CHAPTER 2

Forgiveness

Darling, just fucking own it.

—Anonymous

We all have had experiences of either needing to be forgiven ourselves or trying to forgive others. However, some people, hardheaded people, think that forgetting will be just as good as forgiving. The problem with that decision is that forgetting does not heal, it only covers up the wound, and eventually that wound will become exposed by a memory or a person or a place and then *bam*, there you are, right back where you started, hurting all over again.

I once knew a man who had been abandoned by his father at an early age and raised by his single mother. His father invested in a very lucrative company, and once he became wealthy through his investment, he left his family and spent his money on drugs and women. The man I knew, Tom, resented his father for breaking his promise to his family. Tom vowed to himself never to be like his father. Therefore, at an early age, he valued trust above anything else. Through his youth, he formed a bond not only with his mother but also with a group of friends who had also been hurt. This group of friends, all misfits from broken promises, formed a bond or, rather, a code of brothers. Essentially they became one another's family (imagine *The Godfather*). I think they literally thought they were all gangsters and that trust was everything within their "family." If you broke the trust, you were out of the family. They kept this friend family strong through high school, young adulthood, and even when they started getting married and having children.

Well, as it so happened, Tom ended up getting in some kind of trouble and borrowed money from one of his best friends from that group. He ended up never repaying it, lying about it, and getting booted from "the family." His friends told him that he was no longer accepted and that they would never forgive him.

Meanwhile, Tom's father had lost all his money and women. He had gone through rehab, kicked his habits, and was trying to reconnect with his son. Tom would not have it. He blamed his father for everything bad that happened in his life, especially his last abandonment by his friends. I have no happy ending to this story. Tom still resents his father and refuses to let him into his life, Tom has not spoken to his friends since he lied to them, and he has never apologized. Instead, Tom keeps his ego protected and lives a life hidden behind a shadow of misplaced blame, shame, and regret.

Like Tom, all of us have had terrible things happen to us by people we love. But letting that pain continue to suffer in our bodies and our hearts is only hurting us. It will linger and continue to hurt us until we finally rid ourselves from that pain by accepting the opportunity to forgive. Staying angry at someone who once hurt you creates a sickness in the soul that only you can heal. One of the hardest yet healthiest things to do is to face your fear of forgiving someone by being vulnerable to their reaction. They could say something rude and simply not forgive you, or they could embrace you and apologize for their part. They may not even be alive to have a reaction, but as soon as you accept your responsibility of forgiveness and you put in the hard work of swallowing your pride, you will be released from the torture that holding the resentment has caused you. That way, when you have the opportunity to see that person again or reconnect or be forgiven for something you have done, you are able to move forward because you have healed that part of you, and it no longer will be a source of menace or pain. Easy to say, right? Well, yeah, but also easy to do, because all it takes is action.

I learned this great lesson of forgiveness through my relationship with Paul.

Paul and I met through an online dating service. What caught my attention was his profile picture. His picture was simple. All you could see was his eyes peering over the top of a counter with a look that spoke to me. My reaction to this picture was an instant giggle and a spark of affection for his good humor. He made the first move by posting a waving hand icon. I responded back with a wink icon. From that, a conversation ensued. I found that I was attracted to his sense of humor, his good looks, and the fact that he was also a single father of two kids about the same age as mine. The one drawback to Paul was that he was really short. He was five feet three, and I am almost six feet tall, but that just added to his uniqueness, and it did not matter once I met him in person because by that time, I had already fallen for his personality. We chatted through email, text, and eventually phone calls. He thought my dark sense of humor was endearing. He discovered this sense of humor when I had told him that I had adopted a cat (Fatty) when I had gone to Alaska. I explained that I had brought it home expecting to give it a comfortable end of life. That I added darkly that was three years ago and I had been waiting for it to die ever since. He thought this was hysterical and loved how I was a bleeding heart with a cynical sense of humor.

After the obligatory getting-to-know-you phase through text and phone calls, we decided to meet up in person at the brewery where he worked. Little did I know he had all his friends there at the front watching me as I entered, making sure I was suitable for their friend. He had told me that he was in the back barroom, so I walked through the restaurant anxiously looking around at the waitstaff that all appeared to be staring at me. As soon as I entered the back room, I saw him sitting down laughing with the bartender. The first thing I noticed was his long dark wavy hair and olive complexion. When I approached, he stood up to give me a hug and pull out a barstool for me. I towered over him! I could not believe how short he was. Our looks and height could not have been more opposite. All the men I had been with, including my ex-husband, had at least been my height if not taller. But, after the initial shock, I never really was very aware of our height difference. When I finally sat down, he ordered me a beer that he had helped brew, and we dove into conversation.

Our conversation flowed like the beer flowing into our mugs. We had a great discussion filled with funny stories about work and anecdotal quippets about the joys of being a single parent to young children. We found out that we took our kids to the same day care and that his ex-wife actually worked there. I could not believe that I knew his ex-wife, but we did live in a very small town.

One beer turned into three, and eventually we decided to go back to my place. I was not sure what he would think about my living situation. I lived in a one-bedroom condo, but I had built a wall in the bedroom to separate my children and myself. It was brand-new, and I was the first tenant. It had three decks, a basement that I had turned into a playroom, and a garage. I thought it was nice but was nervous that maybe he would think it was weird that I somewhat shared a room with my children. That was not to be. I later found out that he lived in a very small duplex with a roommate and that he and his kids also shared a room, his son in a crib and his daughter on the top bunk and him on the bottom bunk!

Anyways, we had a lovely night, and he made me laugh so hard. I remember sitting on the futon (the only couch I had at the time) just doubled over in laughter knowing that I was going to end up in bed with this man tonight. And of course, I did. I was pleasantly surprised that our height difference did not make sex awkward. We were actually very compatible.

After that first night, we spent every free minute in each other's company. We eventually got our kids together and took them to parks, for hikes in the forest, and out to dinner as a big group. It was very refreshing. I had found someone that I thought was adorable, funny, and kind. We were very passionate for each other and had the same ideals of how a successful life and family should be. We also both loved to party and were very good at it as well! Now it was time to introduce him to the family.

The first time he met my parents was on Father's Day. His kids were out of town with their mother, and to keep his mind off missing them, he decided that a day on the golf course would be entertaining. This was the first time I had gone golfing with

Paul and only the third time in my life. But hey, I was game for anything.

We rented a cart, and as we drove to the first hole, he proceeded to take his shoes off. I know that I have not been golfing a lot, but I thought having special golf shoes was a thing. But not with this guy. He marched to the beat of his own bongo! He claimed that the best part about golfing was walking in the perfectly groomed grass with bare feet. Who was I to argue? The second best thing about golfing for him was apparently drinking massive amounts of beer and driving the cart like a wild man through the golf course. Thank goodness, he chose the old golf course way out of town that was practically empty.

Nine holes in and we were laughing our heads off, driving like maniacs, and just having a grand old time. Since I was driving home, I limited my intake, but he did not. After all, it was his Father's Day, and he was going to celebrate it how he wanted! Eventually, we made it to the end of the course, and I am sure the few other patrons on the course and the employees as well were glad to see us crazy hooligans finally leave.

When we got back to my place, my parents called and invited us to dinner. They had extended the invitation to Paul, which I thought was very kind, considering they had never met him. I was so incredibly nervous because I knew how my parents were. Paul, on the other hand, was still drunk and not nervous at all. However, reality and nervousness started to set in when after twenty minutes of searching my house and my car, he was not able to find his shoes! After going over all our last movements, he realized that he had left them in the golf cart at the golf course. But that was forty-five minutes away, and there was no time to go get them now without being late to dinner. So we just decided to go, me in my dress and him with grass-stained hairy feet.

Yes, folks, my new boyfriend went barefoot to a restaurant to meet my parents for the first time. Luckily it was an outdoor barbecue place, but still, everyone else had the decency to remember their shoes, but not my Paul, but it gets worse (or better, depending on how you look at it). Not only was he barefoot, but he also had just recently painted his toenails red. You see, my youngest son was really into painting his nails, so Paul painted his toenails in solidarity with my son. Sweet, I know, but now…?

We arrived at the restaurant and noticed my parents' car was already there. We took one last deep breath of courage and walked into the restaurant. I immediately saw my parents standing at the entrance waiting for us. Well, this was it, and there was no turning back. I smiled, gave them a wave, and acted like everything was normal. I walked my barefoot boyfriend up to my parents and made the introductions. My dad, standing at six feet two inches, looked down upon this short, shoeless, hairy man with red toenails and just nodded, twitched his cowboy mustache a bit, and did his best to shake his hand without strangling me or Paul. I could see in my dad's face that he wanted to either grab me by the waist and throw me over his shoulder and out of the restaurant or simply squash Peter with his cowboy boot. But, to my surprise, and relief, my dad held it together like the sophisticated man that he was. He did not miss a beat and acted like nothing was out of the ordinary, although after his handshake, I think I saw a look of repulse cross his face as he made his way to the bathroom to most likely wash the disappointment off his hands. Of course, my mother immediately inquired about the red toenail polish and had no problem bringing all the available attention on the barefoot man in the restaurant. I think she was thrilled to poke fun at him for her own enjoyment.

I really do not remember the rest of dinner because I was pretty much mortified of my situation but was trying to play it off as casually cool as possible. I cannot believe we did that. I would just like to apologize right now to my parents for that terrible encounter. I can just imagine the conversation or argument or hysterical laughter that took place in their car on their ride home.

Paul and I kept going strong in our relationship, and we had gone to my therapist to talk to her about blending families and how to do that in the healthiest way as possible for all parties involved. We were trying really hard to show the world and ourselves that we could do the impossible and make everyone happy. We wanted our children to see that divorced families could still be families. Therefore, that year during Thanksgiving, we decided that we would have my ex-husband and his girlfriend over to Paul's house so that my kids could be with both their parents and their new partners. Oh, how progressive, right? I wanted to host Thanksgiving at my condo, but since Paul had just gotten a DUI (second one for him), he had an ankle monitor and was on house arrest. So we had to have it at his house.

The idea to have my ex-husband, his girlfriend, my kids, his kids, and the two of us together for the holiday was completely crazy at best, but at the time, I thought it was healthy for the kids to see how families could work in all sorts of ways. It was an incredibly awkward dinner, but we made it through and have not done a holiday like that since! Thank goodness!

Paul and I were inseparable. We ruled the blended family world and thought we were incredible. So naturally, we decided to make it official and move in together. After searching for the perfect house to rent for our family, we settled on a darling home right near the children's school. It had a nice backyard and plenty of room for all of us. That March, we pulled the trigger and officially blended our families and were cohabitating. Living together was wonderful, at least for the first summer.

We did everything with such zeal for life and love of adventure. We built an amazing fort in the backyard for the kids, we went on torturous hikes in the forest that were always great teaching moments for at least one of the kids. We had infamous camping trips where we held our annual family "Summer Olympics", we taught the youngest kids to ride their bikes, and we even went on a family trip to Lake Powell with my parents. It was by far the best summer that we had as a family.

Like summer, the fun had to end. It was time to get everyone back to school. Even Paul was going to school. That summer, Paul had decided that he wanted to go back to school and got accepted into our local college to study. Well, now, I have no idea what he was studying. But I digress. He quit his job and got financial aid. I, on the other hand, had finished my master's and student teaching and got a job at the local elementary school where all four of our kids attended. Once school started and things got busy, I quickly realized that Paul was great at having fun, but when it got serious and all the responsibilities demanded attention, he talked a big talk, but did not do much in effort.

I do not know if any of you have gone through this, but being the caretaker/mother/stepmother of four children within the ages of four, five, six, and seven is utterly exhausting! I was responsible for most of the household and parenting duties. I was in charge of getting all the kids to and from school, assisting with homework, cooking the meals, and doing all the bedtime rituals. I also got the kids enrolled in sports, and made sure they had all the gear and showed up to the practices and games. I was doing this all on my own. Paul was doing his homework. He would sleep late into the morning because he did not have to go to school until 10:00 a.m., and he would stay up late "doing homework." By the time he woke up, the kids and I had all had breakfast, got ready for school, and left the house. When we got home from school, he was usually there drinking a beer and possibly doing some homework. It wasn't that Paul was not capable, it was that Paul thought his job was to be a student like the kids and not to be a parent. So he kind of just acted like one of the kids. I also was trying to do everything because I thought I had to prove my worth as a stepmother, mother, girlfriend, teacher, and everything else. I took control of everything because that was what I was trained to do. It was also how I found my own personal value (which now I see is just so sad).

Paul did great in school during his first semester. His teachers noticed his skills and intelligence, and he excelled under their appraisal. But like all things with Paul, he started out with enthusiasm and gusto, but quickly lost motivation and steam and came up with excuse after excuse of why he was failing.

The other issue that I was dealing with was working with our exes. Paul and his ex had a vicious relationship, and they could not speak to each other without ending up in court. So I ended up doing all the communicating and coordinating for both his ex-wife and my ex-husband. This, too, was mentally exhausting. I was trying so hard to please everyone, and it was taking its toll. The other responsibility that I had on my shoulders was paying for the rent and bills. Paul's financial aid did help us, but it was my consistent paycheck that kept us outfitted in a nice house, with good food and family entertainment. Paul provided humor, opportunities to drink, and overall frustration.

I believe it was my control of everything and his feelings of inadequacy that pushed him and me over the edge. He started drinking more and more and started earlier in the day. I did not drink as much during the school year as I did in the summer, and it became a point of contention because he started feeling bad when he continued drinking and would get angry with me when I wanted to call it a night. His anger would last through the night and then just bleed into the next day. He was becoming a very mean drunk. He began fighting with my children because they were getting more of my attention, he punished his kids too harshly, he punched holes in the walls, and he manipulated me to think everything was my fault. The honeymoon period was officially over, and we all started to realize that our situation was starting to crumble.

Paul started getting emotionally abusive. He yelled at me all the time, telling me that it was all my fault for his unhappiness. He would get so angry he would throw things, break furniture, light fixtures, and punch holes in the wall. This anger would turn into hatred, and he would yell at my children and punish his children. Then he would feel guilty and tell me that it was my fault that he acted the way he did. He started making fun of me and how I looked, what I wore, and how I talked. When I would get sad about these remarks, he would tell me that he did not mean to hurt my feelings, and if my feelings were hurt, well, that was of course my fault! He would warp every conversation so that I always thought it was my fault. According to him, it was my fault that he was not doing well in school, that it was my fault that he could not get all his work done on time, it was my fault that he was not passing his classes, and it was my fault that he was unhappy. The worst part was that I started to believe him. I actually thought that everything that was wrong in our relationship was because of me and my lack of, well, everything, I guess. I constantly asked myself, am I crazy, or is something wrong with this situation? I doubted myself and my own moral compass. I started believing that Paul truly did deserve more and that everyone else was wrong and just out to get him. Because of this insanity, life started to get really confusing and uncomfortable for everyone.

We tried our best, but it was becoming a very toxic environment. When the kids were not with us, we drank and argued. When the kids were there, I tried to do my best to appease him so it would be calm and just keep the kids happy and distracted. Eventually, we were all just tiptoeing around Paul so he would not blow up. It was a very confusing time for all of us. I was trying so hard to protect all the kids and make the family work, but doing this was only enabling Paul and his behavior because he would not confront himself or accept any responsibility for his actions. He made everyone feel sorry for him and placed blame on everything in his life except for himself.

Finally, I had had enough, and I decided that this situation was not healthy for me or my kids, and even though I wanted to protect his children too, there was nothing I could do. So after our first Christmas together as a family, I decided that me and my kids were going to move out when our lease was up that March.

It was January when I finally had enough courage to tell him that I could not take it anymore and that my kids and I were going to move out in March. My plan was to stay there and tell the kids during their spring break, because I did not want to disrupt their school or routine. When I told him this, he disagreed and said that there was no reason to wait and to tell the kids at that very moment. I thought this was a terrible idea because we needed time to arrange things, process the change, and make new living arrangements. But he would not hear it. He demanded that we bring the kids out of their rooms at that very moment and tell them that the family was splitting up, and it was all my fault. Since I knew this was irrational and I could sense that he was getting very angry, I called my ex-husband and told him to come to our house and pick up the boys and did the same with his ex-wife. Thank goodness I did that, because what followed was awful!

Once the kids were gone and we had time to talk, he immediately went into a rage. At the time, I was undecorating the Christmas tree, and as he was spewing evil things to me, I grabbed one of the ornaments and threw it at him. This was a huge mistake. As soon as I threw that ornament, he came charging at me and grabbed my shoulders and pushed me into the kitchen and shoved me up against the wall. My reaction was instinctual. I started kneeing him in the balls to get out of his grasp, and that was when I slipped. I slipped on the water that had spilled from the dog bowl and somehow in the process broke my pointer finger. During the scuffle, he threatened to call the police. As he was holding up the phone showing me the number he dialed, 911, I again tried to free myself. He said that my movement caused his finger to slip and push the dial button. He said it was not his fault that the police were called, but rather it was my fault. The phone call was not even answered before he hung up because he knew there was no reason to call the police. But per policy, if the police dispatcher receives a call but is disconnected before answering, they will immediately call back to ensure that the caller is okay.

So of course, Paul's phone rang and it was the police. He answered the call, responded to their questions, and said that everything was fine and that his "girlfriend had just thrown a Christmas ornament at him" but the phone call was an accident. Well, that was all it took, and ten minutes later, the police arrived at our house in response to a domestic violence situation.

When they arrived, they immediately separated Paul and me into different places in the house and proceeded to ask us to tell them our version of what had happened. I explained to the cop how it had all started about me telling Paul that I was breaking up with him. I told him how he got angry and how I had the kids go to their other homes. I then told him how I had thrown an ornament at Paul out of frustration and his response of pinning me up against the wall with his hands on my shoulders. No matter what he had done since I had started the fight by throwing an ornament, the police told me that I was deemed the aggressor and that I was being charged with domestic violence. It is our state's law that if the police respond to a domestic violence call, there must be an arrest made no matter the story or situation. So, I was the one who ended up being handcuffed and put in the police car. Don't get me wrong, I am not claiming to be innocent, I did throw the ornament, but that hardly seemed like a reason to arrest me, especially since Paul had grabbed me and pushed me up against the wall, but hey, I started the fight.

Remember that broken finger? Well, I showed the police my finger, and they decided that it required medical attention. They took me to the hospital to have an x-ray. It turned out that it was broken and they had to put my finger in a metal splint. When I arrived at the jail, I was processed and booked and put in a holding cell until they determined where I was to stay for the duration. It turns out that because of this metal splint on my finger, I was deemed an "armed" inmate, and I was immediately put in the twenty-four-hour lockdown facility with the really hard female criminals.

I still cannot believe that this happened, but yep, it's true, me, this elementary school teacher, who had never been pulled over for a traffic incident, was in the twenty-four-hour lockdown next to these other women who had knifed their husbands, stolen cars at gunpoint, and robbed a liquor store while pregnant. Yep, these ladies were hard, but also as it turns out super nice! They taught me how to make a hammock using my bedsheet and the jail bars, they showed me how to position myself so I could watch the TV that was in the very corner of the hallway, and they all gave their cookies (and made me give all my food) to the pregnant inmate.

Since I was arrested on a Friday night, I was in a twenty-four-hour lockdown for three days because the courts were only in session on weekdays. Finally, Monday rolled around, and I was taken to court. I was escorted by a policeman into the courtroom, and let me tell you, walking into a courtroom in my orange jumpsuit with handcuffs on my wrists and shackles on my ankles was an experience I will never forget and certainly one for the books, well, this book, I guess! On top of all that, when I walked in, I immediately saw my parents, who at the sight of me, started sobbing in disgrace. Then, I saw Paul. He had cut all his hair, shaved his beard, donned a nice suit, and was smiling at me. Seeing him in the courtroom after he had created this whole mess made me infuriated. I looked over at the judge and recognized her last name. The judge glanced at me, then down at her docket and recognized me as her grandson's teacher. She gave me a friendly smile and told me that I was a great teacher and that her grandson loved me.

That may seem a little strange to some, but when you live in a small town and are in public service, you know a lot of people. As a matter of fact, the guard on the night shift also was a mother of one of my students.

My lawyer was great. He explained exactly what had occurred and how it was a simple argument that was blown out of proportion by Paul's aggressive behavior. Then it was Paul's turn. He read from a prepared statement and said, if there was anyone at fault here, it was him. He made a mistake in calling the cops in the first place. He was to blame because he was the one who acted violently, and he also was to blame for my broken finger. The judge did not really care about his statement, just nodded and smiled. She continued through her legal process and asked Paul if he wanted a restraining order placed against me. At this, he simply smiled and acted like he was being very valiant and gracious by saying that it was not necessary. The judge dismissed my case entirely, and I was released to go home!

Yep, this hardened criminal got to walk!

Yeah, I cannot make that up, folks, that happened!

After that adventure, I promptly found a new place and moved out. I cut all contact off with Paul but stayed connected to his ex so that I could still see his children.

My boys and I concentrated on our simple family and started the healing process. I dedicated myself to them and their little boy adventures. We spent so much time outdoors, playing in ponds, collecting creatures, building Lego cities, camping, and making forts. My boys worked hard in school, and I continued furthering my career. After a few failed relationships, well, let's be real here, "casual sexual encounters," I found myself missing the passion that I had with Paul.

Let me just stop here for a bit. Looking back and writing this, I realize how crazy this can all sound. After everything that happened, how could I possibly miss Paul? Well, that's the thing with being in an abusive relationship. The abuser is manipulating their partner to feel like they deserve to be treated poorly, and they do not deserve anything better, and that they will never be loved by anyone else. And I was just as much to blame. I did not love myself, and I thought I deserved his abuse. When I was with him, it never seemed like abuse, rather I was convinced (by him) that he was misunderstood and it was everyone else's fault or madness. I was definitely sick and under some rock where I could not find my head.

During those two years while the boys and I were living peacefully, Paul had gotten kicked out of school, went to counseling, tried to quit drinking, moved to different houses to later find himself homeless living in his car with our dog. Eventually my pity took over, and I started answering his phone calls and texts. Of course, he told me all of his thoughts, and I was right back where I started. I was letting him take over and fill my head with his truths. Eventually I let him park his car in my garage and sleep there. This only happened when my boys were at their dad's. I convinced myself that I was being a good person and just trying to help Paul get back on his feet. Luckily, his mother also was helping, and she let him move into a house she was renting for herself and Paul's half sister.

With him having a place, he started staying with me the weeks my kids were gone. Slowly, like a tapeworm, he worked his way back into my life. He took advantage of the situation and my loneliness and weakness. He soon talked me into believing that he had changed and was much better. He claimed he was not violent, not drinking, and admitted to all his mistakes and bad choices.

At first, I did not bite, but eventually I started letting my guard down and letting him back into my life and my heart. Before I could blink, we were back together and spending time with all the kids together once again. This lasted for a few months, and then he proposed to me and I accepted. Next thing I know, my boys and I were moving back in with him and his kids. His mom and sister and Paul were all living in a house together. His mom and sister got a new place and they were moving out, so I moved into that house with my kids. I know what you are saying, "Wow! That girl is stupid with a capital S," and yes, I would agree. At that time, I was not loving myself, and my brain was filled with chickenshit! I once again was in a relationship with my abuser.

At his worst, Paul was a narcissist and was an addict. He knew how to make me feel responsible for everything, pity his circumstances, and try to solve his problems for him. He knew I had a huge heart and that I was a caretaker. He took advantage of that, and I just kept craving the feeling of being needed.

It took some major pride swallowing on my part to get this family life to work out again. I had to have my parents and ex-husband over for dinner with all of us to explain why we were moving back in together. I had to prove that we were going to be better, that all was forgiven, and Paul was healthy. They grudgingly agreed to support our decision, and that was it, we were back.

By that time, Paul had been kicked out of school and was a brewer at a local brewpub, and I was teaching at the middle school and going to school myself working on my second master's. During that first year back together, we were having fun as a family. As usual, I took care of all the kids during the summer. We would ride our bikes from our house (in town) and go visit Paul at the brewery. Then we would ride our bikes to the river and play in the water. We took the kids up to my family's lake cabin and spent some fabulous time together. But as I am sure you can all predict, these fun times did not last long. That winter, Paul ended up getting fired from the brewery and was unemployed. This was devastating to his self-worth. Here he was jobless, without an education, living with a woman who had her shit together. It really shattered his ego, and this created a self-loathing storm within Paul. He could not deal with the fact that I was working, going to school, and taking care of the kids. He had gotten kicked out of school, fired from his job, and had nothing in the works. He was drinking, not parenting, and being a complete wrecking ball to all of us. I wanted to get out, but I was still being manipulated into thinking that it was all my fault, and I also had my family watching me. After all, I had convinced everyone that I would make it work this time. I could not let everyone down. So instead of giving up, I put everything into the relationship. I took ownership of everything and kept my head down while I worked my ass off and kept the kids and myself out of Paul's way.

During this time, Paul decided once again to go back to school, this time to be a policeman. I know, right? A policeman? After two DUIs, a domestic violence incident, and being an alcoholic. But somehow, he convinced the school to accept his application, and once again, he was in school, and I was keeping everything else together. During this time, we moved into a bigger and much better (much more expensive) house. But it was worth it. The kids loved the house! They each had their own bedroom, a huge toy loft that even had a cool ladder up to it, and a huge basement with an entertainment center. The house was in the woods, and the kids built amazing forts and bicycle courses, and had a great time adventuring in the outdoors.

I was focusing on my career and raising all the children without Paul. Eventually, Paul graduated from the police academy, and he had finally accomplished something. He felt good about it and had rebuilt some confidence. But, unfortunately, this was not to last. Due to his history, not a single sheriff's office or police department would hire him. He applied everywhere, only to be interviewed and then turned down again and again. Being unemployable made him so upset. And once again, his self-loathing turned into a terrible situation for our family.

During the summer, when he was not working, he would sit and drink and watch me work. He would tell me how to lay down the flagstone for the path I was building, or how to clean the chicken coop correctly, but he would not lift a finger. He would tell me what to do with the kids and get angry if I did something else. Then at the end of the night after dinner, he would get infuriated that I wanted to go to sleep instead of staying up and drinking with him.

One night in particular, he was very upset. It was a weekend night, and he had made dinner for us. We all sat down on the huge couch to watch a movie, and he insisted that everyone had made sure to take up plenty of room so there was no room for him. Of course, that made everyone get uncomfortable and scoot over to ensure him that there was plenty of room. There was *no way* four small kids and myself could hog an entire double sectional couch! He ended up pouting and sitting on a stool in the kitchen, sighing and rubbing his back from the pain he was getting from sitting on a stool. We were trapped. No matter what we did or said, he was going to be angry. He just needed a reason, and apparently this was good enough. He got so angry, he started spewing terrible things to his son. I had to cover his son's ears and make him just look at me and ignore his dad. It was really sad. I sent all the kids to the basement with some cookies and instructions to finish the movie and have fun so that I could deal with Paul. When I turned around to face Paul, he had gone into the bedroom, into his closet to get his gun. He locked the door and would not let me in. I heard all kinds of banging, and I started screaming at him to let me in. Finally, he got what he wanted, attention and drama. He opened the door and started throwing bullets at me, telling me that I was not worth a single bullet. I ended up locking myself in the closet to escape his rage and lay there until I could hear him pass out on the bed snoring.

He made life miserable for all of us. But I was determined to keep the family together for the sake of the children (what a crock of shit).

January came around, and he still did not have a job as a policeman but was working a part-time job at a local bakery. Between his failure to get a job in his field, his low income, and watching his family being taken care of by his girlfriend, his world was like an avalanche, uncontrollable and damaging to everything around.

One weekend in January, I had planned a trip to my childhood hometown to surprise my best friend for her birthday. Paul and I and the kids drove for six hours on a Friday night after school to arrive at midnight so we could surprise her in the morning. Upon our arrival, her husband snuck us into the house and into her basement. My oldest son immediately went for the couch because he just wanted to go to sleep. We were all so exhausted. Paul started yelling at my son for taking the biggest couch to sleep on. When I walked up to resolve the situation, I heard Paul yell "You're a fucking asshole" to my son.

I was done. I would not let him speak to my son that way, and of course with urgency, I got Paul into our bedroom. There I told him that this was unacceptable and that he was being immature and inappropriate. He got very angry and started shouting at me. I did what I normally did in these situations. I calmly talked him down, just trying to make the situation less volatile. I told him that we were all tired, it was no one's fault, and that we all just needed to go to sleep. This approach sometimes worked, but this time, he was just fuming. I knew there was nothing I could say or do to calm him down. I decided to just go on with my business and not participate in his anger. I proceeded to get ready for bed. I changed into my pajamas, brushed my teeth, and lay down in bed. To avoid him, I set up my iPad, put on my headphones, and just ignored him while I watched TV. This made him furious because he wanted to keep fighting. He lay down next to me and started poking my shoulder with his finger over and over and over again so that I would engage with him.

I was getting really annoyed with his shoulder-poking strategy, so I told him to stop. I rolled over toward him, nudging my elbow at his hand to stop him from poking me. I then turned my face up toward the ceiling and just sighed in frustration. And the next thing I knew, Paul's hand came down on my face with all his force and anger. I felt a rush of pain in my nose and my teeth where blood was now appearing. I was shocked. I lay there unable to process what had just happened. Paul jumped up and started screaming apologies at me. That was when I realized that he had just hit me. I started crying both because of the pain and also because of the tragedy of the situation. I sat up, walked over to the mirror, and stared at my bloody reflection. I was a mess. Both my nose and my gums were bleeding from the impact of his hand. I quickly walked into the bathroom to control the bleeding and clean myself up. My oldest son and his oldest daughter heard the commotion and ran to the bathroom to see what was going on. There, they just stared at my bloody face in shock. Panicking, they asked me what happened, and this time, I did not cover up for Paul's actions. I flat out told them the truth, Paul had hit me. That was January 13, 2017.

I moved out March 13, 2017. It was the best thing I had ever done. Standing up for myself and my children felt amazing. I took myself and my kids to counseling, and I never got back together with him. I did, however, have to go to court and testify what had happened, which was hard to do and to revisit, but it was necessary.

That was a really long seven years, and it took a lot out of me. But it also taught me a lot about mental illness, the ego, self-worth, emotional and physical abuse, and how to say enough is enough. Moreover, it taught me the importance of forgiveness. Not only to forgive the person who inflicted pain and suffering, but also, more importantly, to forgive myself. After this relationship ended and I had to tell all the children that I failed in keeping the family together, I experienced such pain from my guilt.

I felt guilty for always trying to cover up the awful reality in which we lived so that everyone on the outside would believe that I could do the impossible. I was trying so hard to prove my worth to my parents, my sister, his mother, my ex-husband, his ex-wife, and all of our friends that I was actually hurting myself, my kids, and his kids. I did not want to be a failure in anyone's eyes. But there was nothing I could do. I had to face reality, I did fail, I was not perfect, and this acceptance pushed me over the edge, and I fell into a deep ravine of self-hate and guilt.

All of this guilt and pain hurt me so bad that it took me a really long time to forgive Paul. I wanted to place all that pain and hatred onto him. I wanted him to be the guilty party so that I could come out of this situation unscathed. But for as long as I tried to do this, I could never fully feel resolved because I knew that I also had my responsibilities in that tumultuous relationship and that I needed to forgive myself.

As I mentioned earlier, forgiving someone is a difficult but necessary action. But what I did not say is that forgiving yourself is just as crucial and possibly more challenging. It is a process that needs to be emphasized more often. Its importance is immeasurable. Forgiving yourself is the only way that you are going to be able to make your past your past and not a part of your present. It is the only way that you can learn from your mistakes. Forgiving yourself can only be done by you, and that is extremely hard for people who are codependent on others for their emotions and self-worth. I have just begun learning how to do this, but it has been an incredible journey and opportunity for me. It has helped me find my own self-worth and happiness for myself without depending on others.

So that is what I did. I gave myself a stern lecture. I told myself, "Jeez, Dory, you really fucked some shit up, but I forgive you." I let all my pride go, and I just forgave myself. I forgave myself for letting someone take over my common sense. I forgave myself for dragging four innocent children into that mess. I forgave myself for loving someone more than I loved myself. I forgave myself for trying to fix everyone. I forgave myself for trying to control everything. I forgave myself for not standing up for myself and my children. I forgave myself for being scared. I forgave myself for not listening to myself and trying to convince others of the lies as well. I forgave myself for lying to my mother and father and sister. I forgave myself for enabling Paul to continue drinking and being depressed. I forgave myself for all my actions.

That was a lot of forgiving I had to do, and it was the best thing I had to do, because once I accepted my part in that toxic relationship and forgave myself for my actions and thoughts, I was then able to also forgive Paul. Once I said and accepted all the forgiveness (which did not happen overnight), I felt released from guilt. I was no longer ashamed, and I could look at myself in the mirror again without loathing my everything. I also found that telling Paul that I forgave him for all of his actions and words helped me feel free of the fear of being alone and free of the fear of making the same mistake again.

This lesson in forgiveness was so important for my development because it helped me realize that I am not perfect and I am not always in control, but that I am able to change a situation if I believe in myself and that the only way to do that is to fully embrace every part of me. The ugliest parts of me, my imperfections are the parts that need my forgiveness, acceptance, and love.

The best part about all of those experiences with Paul is that they really helped me figure out what I *do not* want in a partner. It also helped me realize that my children were also able forgive me because they love me unconditionally. Even though I sheltered them from most of the events during that relationship, I felt like a terrible mother, because I was not standing up for myself nor my children.

At the same time, they have also been able to watch me grow, take accountability, change, and take charge of my life.

So *do not wait*. Stop holding on to that feeling of pain and guilt. Stop feeling regret. Stop hating someone for what they did. Who do *you* need to forgive? Then do it already. Forgive them and forgive *yourself* and move on. Learn from it and become a better person through it. Allow yourself to admit your mistakes and give yourself a stern lecture and forgiveness. Let yourself be free from all your hatred toward someone else and toward yourself. Accept yourself and your imperfections and allow yourself to be you.

One way that I have been able to learn my lessons from my relationships and go through the process of forgiveness is by writing a letter to them that I never actually give to them. This process allows me to put so much onto paper that has been weighing on my soul. It also helps me to reach emotions that I had not acknowledged or addressed. I highly recommend that you try this method, if not just to rid yourself of the past, but as a way to accept your responsibility in the relationship and then let yourself go from being tied down to any guilt, remorse, or heartbreak you feel.

Here is my letter that I wrote to Paul.

Dear Paul,

> I was just thinking of the first time that you came over to my condo and stayed the night. We went out on the porch and had a cigarette, and then you decided to put your cigarette out by squishing it into an old planter that just had dirt in it. You then proceeded to pee on it to make sure it was out. I cannot believe that I was not disgusted by this action, but hey, I was raising two boys and had my fair share of male cousins, so it really did not faze me. The next morning when we woke up, we found that the planter had melted all the way down to the bottom and turned into a plastic puddle stuck to the deck.

We laughed so hard because of the stupidity of the situation.

We really did have a lot of laughter throughout our relationship. Blending our family was really exciting as well. I loved watching our four kids all play together and make memories. Do you remember when we lived in the cute downtown neighborhood and the kids wanted to sell apples? They decided to fill the bike kid carrier with apples and go through the neighborhood. But they did not want to walk, so your daughter was on roller skates, your son stood on the back of the carrier, my oldest was on Rollerblades, and my other son was sitting on the apples in the cart. All the boys decided to write "Apples for Sale" on their chests, and the four of them took off through the neighborhood selling apples! I think they sold, like, three before they figured out that riding in the cart and roller-skating in a connected train down the steep street in front of our house was more fun than selling apples. They did that over and over again. The best part happened when I was filming this crazy display of wild youth. You made a paper airplane and threw it to them as they rode down the hill in their wild roller train, and then, your son caught the airplane mid-flight! It was so awesome and funny! What a great moment in life for all of us. These are the memories that I will cherish.

Thank you for that moment. Thank you for all the moments that I can look upon with a smile and feel joy in my heart. And thank you for the bad times too, because they, too, had their worth. One of these times was when I lived in my condo and you hid from the cops in the ditch. It was December, and I had just cut down and decorated my Christmas tree. Your kids came over to spend the night with my kids. They all wanted to sleep in the living room by the tree. They all fell asleep, and you and I ended up fighting. I cannot remember what the fight was about, but the next thing I knew, you were on the floor with a knife threatening to kill yourself and your kids because life would be better without all of this shit. I had to call the police, and as soon as I did, you ran out of the house and hid in the snow somewhere. The police looked for you everywhere and did not find you. They told me to call them if you came back and not to let you in. Of course, you came back, and of course, I let you back in, and we both apologized and cried. Meanwhile, the kids slept peacefully through all of it and woke up with smiles on their faces, never knowing the terrible nightmare that just occurred. Yeah, that one is a hard one to remember, but the reason I brought that up was to tell you that it's okay that that happened, because I learned from it and have forgiven us.

I forgive you for all the horrible actions that took place between us. I forgive you for all the terrible things you said and did to me and our children. I forgive you for making me hurt. More importantly, I forgive myself. I forgive myself for all of my contributions to the downfall of our relationship. I forgive myself for every hateful thing I said to you. I forgive myself for allowing you to treat me poorly, and I hope you forgive me too.

Going forward, I will only spend time in a memory if it is a happy one. I will no longer allow the bad memories to exist in my present. It is the good times and the awesome memories that I will hold close. I can do this because I have forgiven both of us for our mistakes.

Love, me

I'm finally learning to love myself
Better than I have before
And I know that means I'm breaking your heart
Oh, but lover, we were broken from the start
("Oh But Lover," Haiva Ru)

CHAPTER 3

Acceptance

Just remember, I don't chase, I replace.

—Anonymous

I know I promised you a story about redemption, and after the last chapter, you may be like, WTF, this girl is batshit *crazy*. But please continue reading, it gets better, and through all of these stories/experiences, I get stronger and wiser and even a little crazier. So on to my next lesson in my train wreck relationships, the lesson of acceptance.

This lesson was taught to me by my most recent love, Ben. Hold on to your seats because this one is a roller coaster.

Ben and I met through our common friend Paul. Yes, that Paul, my ex-boyfriend. Ben and Paul worked together at a brewery, the brewery where Paul and I had our first date. Ben's girlfriend at the time also worked there. I met Ben for the first time at that same brewery. He and his girlfriend were staying after work having a drink with Paul, and Paul invited me to join them.

The first time I saw Ben, I thought, "Oh my, that man is the most attractive man I have ever seen." I got lost in his clear blue ocean eyes. Then when looking at the woman next to him, I thought, wow, they are perfect for each other. Two very beautiful people with smiling eyes and innocent hearts. Anyways, I was with Paul and falling in love with him, so I was happy. Ben and his girlfriend Katy were also younger than Paul and I. Ten years younger. But that did not matter.

The four of us hung out often, either hanging out at the river drinking beer or camping or playing board games at my place. It was a really beautiful time in my life. Not long after I had met the couple, Ben and Katy announced that they were pregnant. We were very excited for them, but also nervous. They were so young, but Ben had really wanted a family and they had tried to get pregnant, so we were excited for them. Their son, Skyler, was born, and he had a beautiful first year of life with beautiful parents. Unfortunately, that did not last. Ben and Katy struggled with being young parents, making ends meet, and growing up. To help them succeed, they moved in with Ben's parents, but it did not help. They ended up splitting up because Ben had eyes for other women and Katy would not put up with that bullshit. It was a very sad time because Ben and Katy had a shared zest for life, love, and being young. It was also unfortunate because Paul and I no longer had our couple friends and instead we had to watch a beautiful couple and beautiful baby boy go through a hideous breakup.

After their split, Ben started to drink more heavily. Paul and I had him over from time to time, and we were always drinking, but that seemed very normal. We had no idea the dark world Ben had made for himself. He did not see his son very much, he did not want to be alive, and he drank hard liquor for breakfast, lunch, and dinner. No one really knew how bad his drinking was. We all just thought that he liked to party but had it under control. But Ben was hiding a very dark secret from all of us. He was hiding it so well that we were all shocked when we got a phone call from Katy saying that he was in the hospital and had been in a coma for eight days because he tried to quit drinking.

Paul and I were so sad to hear this and felt guilty that we had not realized his struggle and did not reach out to help. But, we had really grown apart from Ben and had not seen him in over a year. We did not visit Ben in the hospital because his family requested that they have few visitors so Ben could focus on his healing. Thankfully, Ben recovered from his coma, and Ben moved away to start living a sober life with the support of his parents.

A few years later when Paul and I were in our sixth year of being together, we heard from Ben. He was still sober and had moved out of his parents' house and moved in with a new girlfriend. He called us to tell Paul that he was going to be a father again. Ben and this new girlfriend were expecting another baby boy. We were shocked, thrilled, surprised, and, overall, very happy for him. We were a bit surprised that he was having another child with another woman in another city. To Paul and me, it sounded a little confusing, but hey, this was his life, he was sober, he had a family, and he sounded happy.

Well, fast-forward a year, Paul and I had just broken up for the last time, and I and my boys were living in a new house in town. I had my freedom and felt amazing. It was summer, and I was living the life of a teacher in the summer. I had a lifeguarding job and was meeting new friends. I played with my kids nonstop and took my kids to the pool, river, lake, camping, you know, having a playful summer life.

One day, I was in town running errands, and who do I bump into but Ben himself. I had heard a rumor that he had left his baby mama and newborn and moved back to be close to his older son, Skyler. I guess the rumors were true, because here he was standing in front of me looking amazing! I, myself, was feeling fantastic and was probably glowing with positive energy. As soon as we recognized each other, we walked right up to each other and hugged. He had always been a fantastic hugger. He was one of those guys who could wrap his arms around you and squeeze you so hard, you just felt safe. As soon as I was in his embrace, I just felt, well, I cannot explain it, I felt like I was lifted off this earth and was floating in a majestic cloud of joy. Unfortunately, the hug ended, and I was brought back to reality, and we unwrapped ourselves from each other. We continued a light conversation and then said our goodbyes but not without telling each other to keep in touch.

As I drove away, I thought, *Wow!* I can not believe I ran into Ben. He looked amazing, and that hug felt amazing. I never even considered dating him. That would be fun. Nah, he's too young and has a lot of baggage. Oh well, at least I got a great hug.

Later that week, I got an IM on Facebook messenger from Ben saying that it was nice to run into me. I returned the compliment, and then he pursued me by asking if I wanted to go for a hike. I immediately responded yes, and it was settled that we would go for a hike that Friday night.

Before the hike, I started thinking about him and his situation. He had one son, Skyler, who lived here with his ex, Katy. Now he had another son, only three months old, living with his ex in Kirkwood. How could he possibly leave a newborn, and what happened? How could I possibly involve myself in such a complicated situation? I chose not to answer those questions and just go with the flow.

That Friday afternoon, the gorgeous infamous Ben pulled up to my house. I could not believe that this was actually happening. I greeted him at the door, and what I got was another great Ben hug! I showed him around my house, grabbed my backpack, and then we set off on our hike. I lived next to a national forest, so we just walked from my house to the trail. He had brought his roommate's dog, and I brought my dog. We walked and talked for hours. We started with just idle conversation, but as we went further and started to feel more comfortable, we started to talk out the details of what had happened between Paul and me and his current situation with his new son Preston and baby mama Sarah. He told me about the complicated situation and how he was pretty much kicked out by Sarah and her mother (whom they lived with). He had described the relationship and turn of events as being very negative with no other possible solution than the present. I really tried not to think about it, but just focused on the energy I felt between us.

When we stopped at the top, he took out some cherries that he had brought to share, and we sat there eating cherries looking at the view. We were sitting right next to each other, and when our legs touched, my nerves lit up with electricity. I felt alive and wanted more. All the way back, I stared at his amazing calves and felt the energy vibrating between us.

After the hike, we returned to my house, and I made him dinner. It was a relief to see that he was still sober, and we talked a lot about the events that led up to his coma and sobriety. I was really taken aback by the mature man he had turned out to be, and how he had really fought hard against his addiction and was winning! A couple of hours turned into many hours, and soon it was midnight.

He said that he needed to get his roommate's dog back to him and that he should leave. So I gave him another hug and a kiss on the cheek. As I kissed his cheek, he slowly turned his head toward mine, and then for the first time, our lips met. Electricity was everywhere, showering my body. I was engulfed in his eyes, his touch, and his lips. I was in a dream, and I never wanted to wake up.

I get chills thinking about this kiss. It was made of heaven's love. This kissing lasted an hour, and my whole body was on fire. Unfortunately, he really did have to get the dog home, so he did end up leaving but not before making a plan to see each other again.

A few minutes after he left my house, he texted me that since he had left his phone in the car, he had fifteen missed calls and numerous texts from his roommate, his best friend (Paul), and even Paul's mother. Apparently, the whole time he was at my house, they had all been out looking for him because he had told them that he was just going for a hike with Lucky (the dog) but not that he would be gone for eight hours. They had been driving around everywhere looking for him and the dog. They had even gone to numerous hiking trails looking for him. They thought he was missing! Everyone was relieved to receive a text from him saying he was okay, but they were also pissed because of the worry he created.

Falling in love with Ben was inevitable and quick. Ben and I went on three dates, and the first night I stayed at his place, we made love. I am pretty sure that the world stopped turning and there was a lightning storm creating currents of unbelievable electricity all around me. I could not breathe, I could not think. All I could do was feel myself melting into this man's embrace and kiss. Afterward, while I was wrapped up in his arms, he told me that he was falling in love with me and had been since the day he first met me seven years ago. I confessed that I felt the same, and when I rested my head on his chest, I breathed in what I thought would be my forever. I felt like I was finally home. Writing this brings tears to my eyes because I can still feel that connection albeit no longer. I can remember the feeling of his heart and my heart holding hands.

Ben was the most gentle, kind, generous, respectful, funny, adventurous, and safe man I had ever been around. He had been sober for two years, and his fight with his addiction was inspiring. He had a stable job and could fix anything. If you needed a flashlight, he could figure out how to make one for you with a stick and an apple. He was intelligent, yet humble. He did anything needed from him in order to be a good person. His respect for elders, women, people of different races and sexuality was incomparable. He adored his mom and called her often. He had an amazing family that was both intricate yet wholesome. He had a heart of gold and could love you all day long if you let him. His hug was the best medicine for anything. He embraced my kids like his own and taught them about how to love life no matter what your circumstance. I could not believe my luck! He was perfect, and he was the most handsome man in the world, and when we made love, it felt like I was literally creating love with him. It was breathtaking, beautiful, adventurous, and full of passion.

For all of his beautiful qualities, he had double the demons. He struggled with what he thought was a weakness for having an addiction. He spoke about how it was his burden and no one else's, and this made it really hard for him to be vulnerable and receive help. He was riddled with guilt for leaving Skyler to get sober, and he hated himself for leaving yet another son. He did not have a high school degree and never thought he could achieve his GED. He thought that he was stupid and would never get a better job. He felt like he had lost some of his personality to his drinking and that he had to fake being happy so all his friends still thought he was the "fun Ben." He did not have a relationship with his own father, and would sometimes cry because he missed him even though he was still angry with him. So as you can see, he had a tortured heart and soul. To me, it was endearing, and of course, I thought that I could fix all his pain by loving him and accepting him the way he was. And so, that was what I set out to do.

The first year was magic. We explored our new world together like we had just been born. Seeing the world with each other was like seeing it with 3D glasses (yes, I know the world is 3D already, but you know what I mean). We went on hikes in the rain, we swam in the river, we snuck into a rodeo and played in the woods, and we went camping and climbed trees. We ate pie on the roof of my sister's house and went to local museums and geeked out with the volunteer tour guide. Everything was inspiring and filled us with joy and laughter. We did everything like we were ten years old again, loving every second of every day with our best friend, each other.

One day, we both decided that my children should see us go on a proper date. So that evening, we played the dating game. He showed up to the house with flowers, chatted with my kids while I finished getting ready, complimented me on my outfit, opened the door for me, and took me on a picnic. We came home early, and he got out of the car, opened the door for me, walked me to the door, and kissed me on the cheek. My boys watched the whole thing and thought it was so romantic and loved how he treated me.

Our next step was for him to talk to each of my sons individually and ask for their permission to ask me to be his girlfriend. He started with my oldest. The two of them took their skateboards and went to the park. While they were out, they talked, and my oldest was thrilled to have his mother date a man that could do cool things with him, like ride skateboards, do cool tricks on bikes, and throw knives at trees (you know, cool boy stuff). So of course, he said yes.

When they returned, he took my youngest son on a walk. Here was their conversation.

Ben: "So, you know that I really respect and like your mother and think she is a wonderful woman."

Son: "Yeah, I know."

Ben: "Well, I was wondering if it would be okay with you if I asked her to be my girlfriend."

Son: "Yeah, I mean, I want my mom to be happy and not just sit in the corner eating crackers with the cats."

Ben "Me too, man, me too [laughing hysterically on the inside]. Cool, thanks, man."

I mean, *really*? Did my son think that I was *that* lame and lonely that when I was alone, I sat in the corner of my house squatting like a squirrel eating crackers with my cats?

The second year was just as great, and we started building a family together. He had moved into my house after only dating for three weeks—*yep, I know, too fast*—but we knew what we wanted. His son was with us on the weekends, and my boys every other week. We were a couple, a family. We were living the dream, being in love, building a family, and starting to dream about our future. One of our future goals was to have some land that we could build a cabin on and really do our thing in nature. We both loved working with our hands and being outside. I knew I wanted chickens, and he wanted to make things out of nature.

Around that time, my mom suggested that I build a house on the lower pasture of their land. I thought it would be amazing to own land and build my own cabin, but at the same time super nervous to be living on my parents' land, literally in their front yard. Ben was thrilled with the offer. He loved the idea of being near family and building a house. So, after discussing this opportunity and all the positive and possible negative consequences, we decided to move forward and build a cabin on my parents' land.

My kids were excited to have a bigger house and to see a house being built just for us. Ben's son was excited to have more space for himself, and it was overall a very fun adventure. My sister happened to live next door to my parents, and she had a large house with a darling one-bedroom lodge that was used as an Airbnb. My sister was generous and offered the lodge to us while we built the house, that way we could save money on rent. So without hesitation, we moved out of my house and into a one-bedroom lodge.

Picture a typical bedroom with a walk-in closet. Well, that was the size of the lodge. It was one bedroom with a tiny fireplace and the walk-in closet. Well, that was actually the bathroom. There was no door, just a wall separating the main room and the bathroom. There were two sinks, shelves, a mini fridge, and a barbeque outside. It was the smallest space I have ever had to share with anyone, and we were sharing it between four of us (five on the weekends). It was also the most precious time with my family because we had nowhere to escape, so we all just had to be ourselves and love one another and work as a team. It was cozy, cramped, and comforting, and I look back on that time with such fondness.

While we were living in the lodge, we spent time on our new land. We built a chicken coop and worked on cleaning up the stream. We planted grass seed and started irrigating. We started collecting firewood and harvesting mint and fruit from the land. We were doing everything we loved and had aspired to do, and we were doing it together. The really beautiful thing about that time was that I had my best friend with me, and we were really living our dream. I was building a life with the person who made me feel loved and alive. We did not argue, we just worked together and built our life.

Finally after four months of living in the lodge, we were able to move into the house. Yes, I know that seems very short for building a house, but what I purchased was a modular, a log cabin kit you might say. It was built off-site, shipped here, and then put together while finishing the inside. It was amazing!

We moved in at the beginning of November, and we slowly adjusted to our new house. Ben cut wood so that we could have cozy fires every night. We snuggled on the carpet next to the fire-place because during the move, we donated all of our furniture and were looking for new (used) furniture. I think this was the last happy Christmas we had together because we were finally doing what we had dreamed. Living in our own house on our own land, with so many outdoor projects waiting to be started.

It was around this time that I started to notice something in Ben that was making him more distant. He was holding on to something that was hurting him, and he would not let me in. When I would try to help him, he would just close down and say that it was nothing and that he was fine. But I knew that he was not fine, I could see him hurting.

In January, he went to go visit his son Preston. Preston was now two years old and about seven hours away in a town called Kirkwood. I knew these trips were hard for him because he did not like to confront his reality and be reminded that he had left his son when he was so young. On several occasions, he told me that visiting Preston was hard because every time he had to leave, Preston would cry and then Ben would cry the entire drive home. He was really starting to feel more and more guilty about leaving and starting to question why he left in the first place. During this conversation, he told me that he had thought about moving back to make things better with his son. But then he said that he loved me so much and did not want to leave our life. So nothing changed, but nothing really got better.

After that visit, I had asked him if I could go with him next time so I could meet his son and his ex. He avoided the question by saying "Yeah, sure, sounds good," but I could tell there was no truth in this. He continued to keep his life with Preston separated from me, and it felt like he had two families that were not allowed to know about each other. Every time he talked on the phone with Sarah or had a FaceTime with Preston, he would make sure that he was in a private place where I could neither see nor hear him. It started to hurt my feelings, but I tried to convince myself that it was okay and that I supported him and his decisions. But in truth, I did not feel okay. I wanted to be involved. I mean, as soon as we moved into our new house, Skyler had a new custody schedule and stayed with us every other week. I was parenting him and treating him like a stepson. It got harder when Skyler and Ben both went to visit Preston and Sarah, and I was still not allowed to go. When they returned and Skyler started talking about Preston and Sarah, I would feel hurt that I could not share this family with Ben. I did not understand. I tried really hard to just be supportive. I made gift baskets for Preston which I gave to Ben to take with him when he visited. I put packages together for different holidays to send to Preston. I even insisted that Ben buy a Christmas gift for Sarah and send it to her.

I could not figure out why Ben was hiding this life from me, or why he did not want to involve me. I kept telling him that I felt like he had a second family and that it was a secret. Ben insisted this was not true, but it was an issue that was getting heavier and heavier.

I told Ben over and over that I wanted to meet Preston and that we could even try to have him come here for the summers and holidays. But he was not willing to ever confront Sarah. He did not want to make her upset. He did not want to stir the pot, and in all reality, he would have rather had me mad at him than her, because after all, I did not have kids with him. I was just sharing my life with him.

Other than this one issue, life with Ben was perfect. We never fought, and when I mean never, I literally mean never. One reason for this was that we really did not disagree on much, and the other was that he really avoided confrontation and was not much of a communicator. He held all his emotions inside, and it was rare to get him to express anything. Regardless, the simplicity of the relationship was a relief, my kids enjoyed his company, and I enjoyed our families being together.

But as time went on, I started noticing more and more that Ben was slipping away. For instance, Ben had always loved taking pictures of the two of us everywhere, and then all of a sudden he just stopped. He also used to love writing our initials everywhere and taking photos of it, but soon he changed to just putting his nickname on everything. He did nothing for our anniversary (our first-date anniversary) and never talked about our future. When I would talk about going camping, he would just kind of nod, and then would make up excuses of why he could not go. He became consumed with his guilt, and he started having more secretive talks on the phone. He talked about being unhappy at work, unhappy with his friends. He started talking about being jealous of people who got second chances, and the worst was that he stopped talking to me about Preston. I knew he was struggling inside, and he would not open up or let me help. So I stayed quiet, supported him through my words and actions, and tried to be strong for him.

I had accepted all of these things because they were part of our relationship, part of him, and I loved him. I thought they were just pains that would heal with time. But I was wrong.

It was summer, and Ben had just planned a trip to see Preston. It had been a while since his last visit because of the pandemic. I was really excited for him, but I could feel some apprehension or tension in his body and his eyes as he was making plans. I felt it got stronger when he left, and then I felt like something was wrong while he was there. Usually on these trips he would call me every night and text me through the day and send pictures. But this trip was different. He did not call or text me until he was driving back home.

It was 5:00 a.m., and he told me that he had just left and was on his way home. I had a gut feeling that something was wrong. I texted him and flat out asked, "Are you leaving me?" and he said that it was hard to explain through text. So I called and he did not pick up. That was when I knew that something was definitely wrong.

Ben had been absent in our life for a while now, but now, I could feel that I had truly lost him. It was at the moment of realization that my heart broke and I heard my body scream and shriek! But it was not me who was shrieking. It was a noise coming from outside. I opened my bedroom curtain and saw duck feathers flying in the road. I put on my shoes and ran outside.

Three of my ducks had been run over by a speeding truck. They were all still alive but very badly hurt. The other ducks that were not in the road were also in a tizzy. I ran to the first duck I saw and picked her up. Her leg was limp, and her guts were spilling from her chest onto my chest. All I could do was sob and run to my mom's house with a dying duck in my arms.

Mom saw me running with a bloody duck in my arms and immediately brought us in to wash off the duck in the laundry basin. As we washed her, we saw that she was not going to survive much longer. In between sobs, I had to find my dad in the house and ask him if he knew how to humanely kill a duck. He nodded and took the duck to help her be free from her pain. As soon as I handed that duck off to my dad and said goodbye, I realized there were two more injured ducks. I quickly ran back to the road and found the second injured duck. I picked up this one and brought it to my mother's wash basin. This one seemed to be in better shape and its legs were all working, so I cleaned it up and just held it for a very long time, trying to figure out what to do. Eventually I decided to put it in a comfy spot in the coop to see if she would make it through the day. The third duck was not injured and was able to escape the murderous truck. As soon as all the ducks were taken care of and my adrenaline finally started to return to normal, I collapsed in my mother's arms and just sobbed.

My mom thought that I was upset about the ducks, but then I told her about my text with Ben. Then she understood and held me tighter.

Ben was leaving me, I just had my duck bleed to death in my arms, and I had another duck that was suffering that needed to be put down.

Before I continue, I think it is important for you to know that I am a sucker for animals. I once stopped in the middle of traffic to go out on the road and pick up a half-alive groundhog, only to bring him to humane society so he could be euthanized. I cry whenever an animal is hurt in a movie, fake or real, even if it is a damn cartoon! So losing my ducks in this way was really torturous, especially considering the other horrible life event that was quickly becoming my new reality.

That evening, when Ben pulled up, I immediately had him get the duck from the coop and humanely kill it. I needed him to take care of some of this shit that happened while he was gone. When that was over, he came into our room and calmly told me that he had decided to move back to be with Preston. I was devastated.

He told me that he regretted leaving Preston three years ago and wanted to be a better dad. He did not want to repeat the same mistakes his own dad made. He said that he wanted to prove to himself and his sons that he could provide for them on his own. Who was I to argue with a father trying to do the right thing? My heart was ripping open, but all I could say was that I supported him and was proud of him for taking this chance and opportunity to be a better father. However, in doing this, he was once again abandoning one of his sons. This time, it was Skyler. For the first time in Skyler's life, he was with his dad every other week rather than just weekends or holidays. Skyler was so happy to finally be living with his dad. But since he was ten years old and Ben had lived away from him before, Ben thought that Skyler would be just fine with him leaving again.

Without much to say, I told him he could have two weeks to move out and that he could stay here during that time and slowly pack his things. Yeah, I know what you are thinking, well, maybe. You are either thinking, wow, that girl is a sucker, or wow, she is way too nice. Well, you are right, I am both of them. I am a sucker for love and trying to be the best person I can be, and I am also too nice. Everyone told me to kick him out, to not let him have the help in moving, to show him no mercy, no compassion. But that was not me. I was the better person. I was the person who could be beat up but not shed a tear. I was the person that would love unconditionally. I was mature, I could handle it. So I fought my emotions, helped him pack, was polite all day long, and fell apart in my room every night.

Heartbroken and feeling unworthy of his love, I fell into a deep valley of sorrow. I would write in my journal a lot, something I had not done for years, but found therapeutic. I drew a picture of a deep ravine, like the Grand Canyon, and I drew a picture of myself lying facedown at the bottom, arms and legs bent in odd angles, dust all around me, and nothing to suggest any sign of life. That was how I felt. I felt shattered again, like I had in the past. But before, like at the end with Paul, I had been excited to pick up the pieces and rebuild myself. This time was different because it was the first time ever that I had *not* been the one to leave. I had always been the breakupper, never the breakuptee. I've never felt so alone, unloved, and pathetic. It was dark.

During those two weeks of him staying here but preparing to move, my cousin, her husband, and their young girls came out for a visit. It was a preplanned visit, and it was their only vacation that summer, so I could not cancel on her. Plus, she is my closest friend other than my sister, so I thought it may be helpful to have her here. During those last two weeks. Ben slept on the couch and was gone by the time we woke up and would come back home in time for dinner. He would eat dinner with us, and that was awkward, but I wanted to be civilized. I had to keep a smile on my face for my guests and my children, so I just ignored my feelings and was a smiling robot for the week. My cousin and her family left on a Friday, and Ben had planned on leaving that Sunday. So we had the weekend alone to say our goodbyes.

I do not remember much about that weekend because I finally just let my feelings loose. I did not try to protect Ben from seeing my pain. Sunday morning I woke up with blurry eyes, swollen from sobbing all night. Ben was already up and getting ready to leave. I gave him a huge hug and cried into his chest. He stayed stoic. I waited for him to say something, anything, but he did not speak a word. He just let go of me, walked out the door, and drove away. I broke down hard and lost myself. I texted him and asked why he did not say anything, and he said that he did not know what to say, then he texted, "We had some great times." WTF? Was that some kind of a joke? That is the kind of thing you say to someone you casually dated for a month. *We had some great times!* No! We lived a life, made a family, built a dream house, and had found our soul mate!

Splat! I was at the bottom of the Grand Canyon again, and I stayed there for weeks. I started drinking a lot and started smoking again (an old habit from college days). I did not leave the house, I did not eat, and I did nothing but drink and smoke and cry.

I found out that he had parked our pop-up camper on a buddy's property in town and had planned on moving back in with Preston and Sarah when he saved enough money. He texted a bit about how he still loved me and missed me, but I found out from his mom that the very next day after he moved out from our house, Sarah and Preston had come to visit. A little suspicious, right?

I continued my drinking and smoking and not eating and started running more. I lost some weight and started feeling skinny and therefore felt a fake sense of self-confidence. I felt good about the way I looked, good enough to rock my bikini. I tried so hard to get out of the house, go to the river, go on runs in town, ride my bike on the river path, and just try to have some sort of life.

I continued to write in my journal to process my thoughts. I drew my Grand Canyon again. This time there was a tiny tree root peeking out from the side of the canyon. I drew myself holding on to that root with two fingers while the rest of me dangled into the abyss. I felt like I was trying to climb straight up a cliff to get out of the canyon, but with a small breeze, that root would break and I would plummet back down to the dusty bottom.

About a month later, I was riding my bike down the river trail to get to the swimming pool. In order to get there, I had to ride right in front of Ben's work. Of course, on this particular day when I rode by, Ben was standing right above the trail staring down at me. When I looked up and caught a glimpse of him, my heart exploded, and I nearly crashed my bike into the railing. He walked toward me, and then after saying hello, he told me that he was moving back to Kirkwood the next day. Stumbling over my words, I managed to say congratulations with a pitifully lying smile and took off on my bike. I rode and rode and rode until I could not pedal anymore. I jumped off my bike and threw off my shoes and plunged into the river, into the rapids, and swam like hell to cross to the other side. With all the extra adrenaline I had, I made it to the other side and climbed out to sit on a rock. There, I let my sorrow wash over me and consume me. I lay on that rock crying, gasping for air, but also relieved. He was finally leaving. I did not have to worry about bumping into him again. I did not get to think that maybe he would change his mind. I had to let go. I had to accept it, Ben was gone.

Letting go, what a concept, something that I no longer believe in, but at that time, I thought I had to let him go. So I did the usual. I saged my home, ridding his presence from my life. I wrote angry, awful things about him in my journal. I deleted him from my contacts in my phone. I did everything to make sure I would never talk to, think of, or speak of him again. Of course, this did not work, but it was what I did at the time.

A few weeks after he moved, he told me that he found an apartment and that he needed a "landlord" as a reference and asked if I would be his landlord reference. Being the kind person that I was, I said yes.

A few weeks after that, he texted me and told me that he needed his passport and that he had forgotten it in my safety box. I told him that I would send it, but he told me that he could not give me his address. Hmmm, that was weird, I thought. After what seemed like millions of texts back and forth, I finally got the real reason for this oddity. He told me that he had moved in with Sarah and Preston.

I was stunned. This whole time he had convinced me that he was leaving me to be a better dad, to prove to himself and his family that he could provide for his family on his own and that he could stand on his own two feet. That he loved me but had to do this, that he had no feelings for his ex and had no intention of going back to her. I had believed that and supported this decision, and now I found out he had been living with his other family for a month now.

Well, there I was again, falling off the cliff, falling fast and landing flat on my face that shattered into a million pieces at the bottom of the ravine. He had left our family and moved right back in with his old family within fifteen days.

There it was, he was back with his family, and I was all alone. Completely alone. My kids were spending a lot of time with their dad, and I had no one. For the next few months, I was unable to feel. I was just going through the motions of life without any happiness or reason.

About three months later, one of my cousins experienced real tragedy. Her autistic nonverbal son and her husband were both killed in a fiery car crash. Talk about loss. My parents and I drove twelve hours to go to the memorial. During that trip, I was listening to music on my phone and thinking about my cousin when I got an unexpected text from Ben. He started by saying that he was miserable. That he had made the biggest mistake of his life, that he should have married me when he had the chance and that I was his soul mate and his best friend. He continued and said that he needed to tell me something. Okay, my imagination went crazy. I thought of all sorts of things that he may need to tell me, and then I came to the conclusion that whatever it was, was probably a lot better than what I was imagining. I asked what it was and he told me. I thought my imagination was dark and hurtful, but what he told me beat up my imagination with a baseball bat. Sarah and Ben were pregnant. Yep! He was having another baby.

I dropped my phone and felt like I had fallen from an airplane with no adrenaline but with a fifty-pound weight attached to my backpack. How could they be pregnant? He told me he did not love her, he told me… He told me lies.

I did not respond for a while so that I could process what he said. I did not know what to say back. Congratulations? Ever heard of birth control? How did this happen? And then it hit me, it's November. He moved in August. When did they get pregnant? To find out the truth, I asked him how far along she was. Silence, more silence, and then he was writing. My heart was pounding, and I was clenching all my muscles. She was fifteen weeks pregnant.

Science and math broke through that text and shot into my brain. He had gotten Sarah pregnant when she came to visit him the day after he moved out of our house.

And there you have it! He did not wait one day to have sex with his ex, the one that apparently he had "hated," and the one that had apparently "hated him." They were living together and pregnant. He literally left one family to start another one in one day.

I am pretty sure my heart stopped. Here I was heading to a funeral for my cousin who was suffering more loss than I can imagine, and I found out this news. Enter robot Dory, here she is again, smiling, comforting, empathizing for my cousin on the outside, and feeling charred on the inside, but guilty for feeling bad for myself when I needed to comfort my cousin. It was a very strange trip, to say the least.

When I finally got home, I just lost it. I felt nothing. I continued my drinking and smoking, and good lord, now the holidays were approaching. Life sucked! But I had to get out of this. I had to be a good mother, to stay strong, to work through this, and I knew it would take time and some serious self-ass-kicking.

So that was what I did. Well, not until after Thanksgiving. That holiday was the worst! But after that, I just decided to fuck it all! Focus on my kids and fuck love! I started finding inspirational quotes from Pinterest about not giving a fuck, and I put them on my bathroom mirror, my bedroom walls, my treadmill, and my work space. I found all my pictures of Ben, and I tore them up. If they were digital, I deleted them. I had dance parties by myself on Friday nights, I listened to music constantly, and I worked myself to the bone on fighting for my life and my happiness. And slowly, very slowly, I started to feel better. I started to accept his decisions and his life, and I started to accept mine, even though it was not what I wanted. I started accepting my situation and my future. I *had* to accept and forgive Ben and myself so that I could start living again.

This time I was the one fighting for me. If no one else was going to do it, well, I better do it! I accepted all of his shit for the time we were together, and I accepted him for those imperfections, and I knew that he was tortured. I accepted all of what he did to me because I loved him. This love continued, and I accepted that he moved on quickly and started a new family. I accept the fact that he continues to this day to tell me through text that he regrets it all. That he fucked up everything. I accept it all because it is the only thing I can do. There is no point in getting mad at him. I loved him, I never wanted to change him because I knew that I am no wiser than anyone else and that I have no right to change anyone, so my only choice was to either accept him or not be with him, and I chose acceptance.

It took a long time to fully accept what he did at the end of the relationship, but I can proudly say that I did. And it feels good. Yeah, it still makes me sad, but not mad. It happened and there is nothing I can do about it, but accept it and move on.

Because of this peace that I found through acceptance, I have been able to stay close to his family and him. I have been able to maintain my own self-respect by not turning the whole thing into an ugly fight. I did not say anything I regretted, nor did anything I would regret. I just let it be. It is the only way that I have been able to truly be free and move on. Holding on to anger or jealousy would just bring me down, and I don't want that. I choose to move on. Therefore, I can honestly say that I do not regret this relationship in any sort of way because it taught me how to not only accept others for who they are, but also more importantly to accept myself.

It was through accepting his flaws that I was also able to accept the flaws within me. I learned how to accept the dirty, the ugly, and the imperfections that I always thought people would hate about me. But after accepting everything he did, I was able to embrace my imperfections and not only accept them but also start loving them. I started thinking about the reason and motivation behind some of my decisions.

For example, at the time of the breakup, I had applied and been accepted into a program to get my administration license so that I could be a principal or work at the district level. I cannot think of one thing that I would like about this type of job. The thing I love best about my job is the relationship that I have with my students. They make me laugh, I made them laugh, we form bonds, and I watch them learn. I would hate being a principal or working for the district. It would take all the fun out of my career. So why did I apply for this program? That's easy, I needed to prove myself to other people, to my parents, to my colleagues, to Ben, to Skyler, to Skyler's mom, to Paul, to Ben's ex. Anyone, and I just needed to prove that I was smarter and better than them.

How ridiculous, right? To go through life trying to prove your worth to everyone else just because I needed to be better than everyone? It was the same thing that I did with my ex-husband and his wife. I needed them to think that I was incredibly kind, generous, and selfless. I would always buy presents for their birthdays, Mother's Day, and Father's Day. I always let them have their way in any disagreement we had about the kids. I always paid for whatever the kids needed because I did not want to ask them in fear that they would be angry. I wanted to have the perfect co-parent relationship so everyone would see that I was amazing.

I tried to hide the real me. I did not want my parents to know that I liked watching TV in the middle of a Saturday afternoon. I literally would shut my blinds if I was planning on watching TV during the day so my parents could not see. If one of them happened to knock and walk in, I literally turned red in the face with embarrassment and shame. It was disgusting! I did not want them to know that I was smoking cigarettes or drinking beer. I thought they would think of me as a lazy, unhealthy person. I mean, I cared so much about what other people thought of me that it was ruling my life. I had no idea that people could accept and even love the real me.

That was until I started reflecting back on how I felt about Ben's actions. Yes, I was hurt, and yes, I wished it had not happened, but I had accepted it because I loved him. So if I could accept that, then I should be able to accept me and my imperfections. Better yet, I should be able to love them. I knew I had to start being more authentic and let everyone else see me just the way I was and either accept or not accept me so that I could get on with my life.

That is exactly what I did. The first thing I did was I un-enrolled in the administration program. And then, I told my parents about it. I was starting to explain to my mother about my choice, and then I just had to stop and think, do I really need to explain this to her? Or do I just want to tell her and then not give a fuck about what she thinks? Well, I chose the latter. And you know what? She was really disappointed, but this time, I was okay with that. I was okay with that because I knew it was the right choice for me. It was incredible, the feeling of making a choice on something really huge by only considering what I wanted.

The next thing that I did to make myself happy was I finally told my ex-husband what I thought was right for the kids. I told him that I would no longer appease him and that I was just going to do what I needed and that if he did not like it, well, fuck it, too bad! His response was nothing. His silent shock made me giggle on the inside, and the respect I have earned from him and my kids because of that has been amazing.

The last thing I needed to do was come clean to my parents about my new smoking habit. It actually happened inadvertently when I was going for a horseback ride with my dad. He said something in the middle of a conversation like, "Yeah, and you need to quit smoking all those cigarettes." I was kind of surprised that he knew, but I did not show it. I simply said, "I'll quit when I want to quit, and I'll quit for myself and not to make you happy. Right now, I love smoking, so get used to it." It felt amazing to come clean, to own up to what I was ashamed of, and just embrace my imperfections and insecurities. I was free.

So yes, Ben was a hard breakup, and all the things he did were terrible, hurtful, and, overall, pretty nasty, but through my acceptance of him and his behavior, I was able to accept the parts of me I was trying so hard to hide. The freedom I have found in just being happy and not giving a fuck about what other people think of me has been so uplifting. As long as I am doing what is acceptable to me, then fuck what others think. If they truly love me, they will accept it too.

I must add a note in here about knowing how much is too much to accept. The point of acceptance is for you to look inside and start accepting the parts of you that you thought were ugly and imperfect and unlovable. Accepting others' imperfections does not mean looking past their bad behavior. If there is something that your partner is doing that is wrong, you do not have to accept it and you should not. Do not accept people's bad behavior if it is dangerous or toxic, or in any way hurting you. If you cannot accept someone the way they are, then move on. And really, move on. You are never going to change anyone but yourself. So if you are like me and have had this thought, "Oh, they are so wonderful, and if I am with them, they will definitely start to do this and that and will be so perfect," well, I hate to say it, but this is a bad situation. *Do not* try to change anyone! Again, if you cannot accept their imperfections, then they are not the one for you.

So, stop waiting to accept yourself and start doing it now. It took me way too long, but now that I have done this work, I am so happy for the experiences that brought me here. Start asking yourself, what is it about you that you try to hide? What part of you are you ashamed about? What are you trying to prove? Wouldn't it just be easier to stop hiding and just be you? What about your partner? What is it that bothers you about them? Can you just accept this action or behavior? If no, then why are you in that relationship? Start being honest to yourself and to those around you. Let yourself be free. The only thing holding us back is ourselves. Start being nicer to yourself, start loving yourself, and be the real you. It is so much easier than hiding behind your fakeness. It's as liberating as taking off your extremely tight, uncomfortable bra at the end of the day! *Folks*, let yourself be free! Accept who you are and move on already!

Here is my letter of forgiveness and acceptance to Ben.

Dear Ben,

I do not regret meeting you because you brought so much joy and laughter in my life and the lives of my children. The adventures we had together were amazing. The camping trips, the road trip to Tahoe, living in a one-bedroom cabin while building our dream home, raising baby chickens and baby ducks together, blending our families, and laughing every night before we went to sleep. These were such beautiful times for me that I look back at them and smile. There is also a pain that reaches deep inside when I think of you because our friendship and love was so unique that it is hard to imagine finding that again. But I know I will because I deserve to be loved and to be in love.

One thing that I really loved about you, Ben, were your imperfections. I really embraced the parts of you that not a lot of people could love. I loved the smell of your stinky armpits after a hard day of work. I loved the way you would sit on the couch, oblivious to everyone, and have your hands down your pants and your belly sticking out, then you would realize that I was looking at you and you would just smile a cheeky grin for being caught. You were so authentic with me, it made me feel accepted. I loved how you had struggled with addiction and were working so hard on overcoming it even if that meant you chewed tobacco or smoked. I loved that you worked at a mediocre job but you thrived in it because you put your best into it every day. I loved your tortured heart and your feelings that you could never express or talk about. I loved you truly for everything and only wanted to help but not change you.

This unconditional love for you was only possible because you let your true self shine to everyone. You did not hide behind the facade of who people or society wanted you to be. You embraced yourself and let yourself be your true self without shame. This is how I want to be and what I have learned from you. I have learned to accept my own imperfections through accepting yours and the challenges you brought to our relationships.

I never wanted to change you because I accepted what you brought to our relationship even if some of it was ugly. I accepted the fact that you had two baby mamas in two different cities. I accepted the fact that you did not want to share one of these sons with me because you yourself did not know him well enough. I accepted your tortured heart. I accepted your addictive behavior. I accepted your need to be loved so much because you doubted your self-worth. I accepted all of your behaviors. Through this acceptance, I learned to accept and embrace my own self and everything that I am.

I now accept the fact that my self-worth does not depend on what my parents think of me. I accept that I have two master's but not the PhD that my mother wanted me to have. I accept the fact that, yeah, sometimes I like to smoke and drink beer on the weekdays even though my dad thinks it is shameful. I accept my job for what it is, I know I am very good at it, and I do not need to prove it to anyone else but me. I accept my failed relationships. I accept any failures I have had as a mother. I accept my difficult relationship with food. I accept my need to be loved and to be in a serious committed relationship. I accept my willingness to still be your friend and respond to your texts and listen to you when you need a friend. I accept all of my imperfections.

More than that, Ben, I love those parts of me. I love the bad, the ugly, and the mistakes because they have made me who I am. This is my life and I am living it, and you have helped me do that by being imperfect and letting me love you just the way you were. Now, I have transferred that love to myself and my own imperfections. Those are now the qualities of me that I am proud of because they make me an amazing fucking awesome woman!

So, thank you, Ben. Thank you for loving me for who I was, thank you for letting me love you and all your imperfections. Thank you for leaving and making me grow and learn to love myself. The day you left, I started telling myself that I was worth it and I was worth fighting for. Now I do not have to say that, because I know it. I believe it. Thank you for helping me get here.

Love, me

Even though I'm glad I met you,
I regret the bitter taste
of not having you,
it feels like a nightmare...
Please don't say anything,
I need you just to know
that I'm missing your soul.
("Wind Up Space," 1010 Benja SL)

CHAPTER 4

Know Your Worth

Because it's my life and that is all
the fuck you need to know.

—Anonymous.

Do you know your worth? Do you ever feel like you are worth more than what other people have shown you? Well, I certainly have had my moments when I doubted myself, sold myself short, and sometimes even thought that I was not worth a particular person's respect. That was surely silly! Of course, I am worth their respect, and so are you! What I am trying to say is that you and I, well, we *are worth it*! I had to write this on my bathroom mirror after many breakups because I started to feel like I was not worth anyone's love. I would say, "Well, if I am worth it, why the fuck are you not choosing me? Where is the proof?" Actually I would yell that and then break down and cry! No more, folks! I know my worth, and who taught me that but my high school boyfriend who most recently came back into my life. This is a fun one, so get ready for some giggles.

Carter just moved to town. He was a senior and I was a junior in high school. Through all of my elementary and middle school years, I was awkward. I had buckteeth, then a headgear, then braces. I was kind of pudgy and getting really tall. I was a real dork and did not have many friends. But in my junior year, I started to grow into myself. I had long blonde hair, and I was reaching five feet eleven. I played volleyball and ran track and started to slim down.

One day as I was walking down the hall, I saw the new boy that everyone had been talking about. He was a skinny punk and had strawberry blond hair that stuck straight up and sideways. I just stared at him, instantly enchanted by his baggy jeans, his punk rock chain, and his cute smile. He was one of those guys that smiled with his eyes as well as his mouth.

Since he was new, he did not have many friends, and that was an advantage for me because if he were popular, I would not have stood a chance. I am not sure if he noticed that I was staring at him every day, or even if he knew that I existed, but sometimes, I think I caught his eye and he would smile at me.

Since I was sixteen and had a car, my parents made me get a job, and I was pretty happy about that. I applied for a job as a hostess at a local hippie restaurant in town. One night when I was working, I went back to the kitchen to drop off the dishes, and when I looked up at the dishwasher, I was stunned to be looking straight into Carter's eyes. He made some funny joke about working there, and I giggled like Tickle Me Elmo! As I left the kitchen, I was dumbfounded with my luck! I worked at the same place where Carter worked. Maybe, just maybe, I could flirt with him and get him to like me.

I loved going to work. I would get so excited to walk into the kitchen like I was on a mission to get something I obviously did not need just to see if Carter was working. He later told me that he requested to have all the same shifts as me. So obviously I got to see him every time I worked.

I remember that I would dillydally at the end of my shift just to make sure that I would walk out the door at the same time he did. Sometimes we would stop and chat at my car, and sometimes those chats lasted longer than they should have, and I would get in trouble for being home late.

The restaurant we worked at was located near the waterfall at the north end of the town lake. It was a really big waterfall, and it was also just a huge cement dam. One night after work, we were talking by his car, but it was getting really cold. Remember, we were in a mountain town in Colorado, so our winters were really cold. As we sat there shivering, Carter asked if I wanted to sit in his car by the waterfall to stay warm. Of course, I did! Duh! As we sat there, I started to get nervous because I could feel the romantic tension that was fogging up the car. I started to shake and shiver. I could not get my legs to stop shaking. Thank goodness, it was cold because I was able to just claim that I was cold. To keep me warm, he put his hands on my legs, and when I was looking at the waterfall talking about how I hated my nose, he leaned over, said he loved my nose, and kissed me. My first kiss. I wish I could say that this kiss turned into a ten-minute passionate kiss infused with desperate teenage lust and love, but I cannot.

As soon as he took his lips off mine, I freaked out. I opened the car door and half stuttered and half screamed that I was late and I had to go. I got in my car and zoomed away. We did not have cell phones then, so I could not text an excuse, so instead I had to live with the dreadful thought all night that I may have just ruined everything I had flirted for with that ridiculous prude move. Lucky me, Carter thought it was cute, and the next day at school, he handed me a note about how the kiss was amazing and that he couldn't sleep because he was thinking about it all night.

Aweeeee, he was so cute! I was so lucky, I actually found a really cute, sweet guy in high school, and he actually liked me! After that night, we got closer and closer and started talking every day.

Our first official date was so weirdly perfect. A girl from my volleyball team invited me to go bowling with her and a group of her friends. I was not really close to her, but she had some classes with Carter, and she told me that they were friends and that she would give me some details about him. I took the bait and could not wait to ask her about him, especially to find out if he talked about me!

We talked about Carter the whole drive there, but she was the one asking questions, like, if I liked him, did I think he was cute, etc. It was really frustrating, but at least I was able to spill all my teenage lovey-dovey shit to someone. Little did I know that Carter was listening the whole time!

Carter had instigated the whole thing and had planned it all out. He thought it would be cool to hide in my friend's car trunk, listen to our conversation, and then pop out and surprise me when we got to the bowling alley.

Well, he was right, he surprised the shit out of me when my friend opened her trunk to "get her extra socks." The surprise of seeing him and thoughts of romance quickly vanished when I realized that he had overheard everything I said about him. But luckily his plan had backfired. Thankfully, the trunk was not conducive for hearing anything but the tires on the pavement and rattling of mufflers.

Bowling was a blast. Even though I was nervous to be around the boy I had a major crush on, I also loved making fun of myself, and bowling was the perfect activity for that. The two of us were just two dorks on a dork date dorking out in the bowling alley.

After bowling, we all went to McDonald's to get some food. Carter ordered a happy meal so he could get a free toy. I ordered a Diet Coke so I could get zero calories. His toy turned out to be one of those troll dolls that were popular in the nineties. You know, the ones that were as big as my pointer finger with troll face features and long hair that stuck straight up. I remember this troll very distinctly because we played with it forever in that McDonald's, laughing so hard at the hilarious ridiculousness of the whole date.

The memories of that date bring me a perma-grin that makes my dimple on my cheek hurt. I cannot stop smiling when I think of those times. They were so magical and innocent.

The date was on a Friday, and that weekend, I talked to him on the phone for several hours. Monday rolled around, and at the end of the school day, I went to the locker room to get ready for volleyball practice. When I opened my locker to get my gear, I saw a red-haired troll sitting on my kneepads with a note attached to it. I did not care how he got into my locker or even what the note said, I was in love.

Every day after that, he would leave me silly notes in my car, he would watch me practice volleyball, and on the weekends, we would go to the forest and kiss for countless hours. So here we were two nerdy lovebirds. He taught me about punk music and smoking cigarettes. He took my virginity and also my heart. He was as much obsessed with me as I was with him.

What a wonderful time in my life. My parents even liked Carter. They did not like the fact that he was from Texas and could not drive in the snow, but Dad quickly fixed that problem. One night after dinner, Carter was trying to leave from our driveway, and instead of going up and out, his car decided to slip down and slide sideways. My dad could not stand this poor performance, so he huffed and gruffed and put on his snow boots and jacket. He marched outside and let himself in the passenger door of Carter's car and proceeded to teach Carter how to drive in the snow. They were out there for hours, and at the time, I think I was embarrassed, but Carter wasn't. He drove away that night with a smile on his face and confidence in his new driving skills.

That spring, Carter was set to graduate. I remember the dress I wore to his graduation. It was a terrible black dress with daisies all over it. I still have the photos. After the ceremony, his parents took him and me out to dinner, and since it was his choice, he chose a weird steak house and, of course, ordered the strangest thing on the menu, rattlesnake. In order to impress his dad, I, of course, tried the rattlesnake to prove my badassness!

That summer was full of punk rock concerts, make-out sessions in the woods, and long conversations on the phone. We both knew that soon he would be moving to Rosewood to attend college, and we were both scared of the long distance between us. After all, this town, though still in Colorado, was a good six hours away. We decided that we would try to stay together, but that we would both give each other space and time to do their own thing.

The day that his family and he were driving to Rosewood for the momentous off-to-college move, I was in tears. We were both in tears. I helped him pack his car, and before he left, we tearfully kissed each other, making promises to talk that night and every night afterward.

The first few days were fine, but Carter, being who he was, made friends quickly and found a new life. I was not surprised, but I was devastated when he started missing our nightly phone calls. I do not remember much during this time, but I do remember feeling hurt but also a bit free. Even though I loved Carter, I was now a senior, and I wanted to explore my own life.

I was playing volleyball, running track, and I got my braces off. I started getting thinner and was growing into my own beauty. I was making new friends and enjoying my time. Just as I was starting to get comfortable in this new experience, Carter contacted me and told me that he was moving back home.

His college career lasted one semester because he flunked out due to partying too much. So the second half of my senior year, he was living back at home, and we resumed our relationship. But this time it was different. I was just starting to find my freedom when he came back into my life being a full-time boyfriend.

Things started getting complicated. I wanted to have a boyfriend, but I also wanted to continue my self-exploration. It became very complicated. I continued to do my own thing, and he became very needy of my time and jealous of me. Eventually he started dating other girls, and I became jealous. Typical high school relationship!

So on it went like this through my last semester of school and during the summer, but we both knew that life was going to change drastically as soon as I went to college. And it did. It did not take long for me to let go of my high school boyfriend and our strained relationship once I got to college.

I bumped into him a few times after that, once at a snowboard shop I worked at during Christmas break, and I even invited him to my twenty-first birthday party. I remember the last time I saw him, I was engaged and at the grocery store in our hometown with my mom. I saw him in the aisle and lit up with joy! We said hey, went through the typical pleasantries, and then I told him I was getting married. He congratulated me with a hug, and then I whispered in his ear, "You were always the love of my life." He looked at me, then whispered back, "Let's promise each other that if we are both alone and miserable at thirty that we get back together." We smiled in agreeance and walked away. That was twenty years ago.

Life went on, I got married, had two kids, got divorced, had relationships, and just continued living. Then once when I was with Paul, Carter found my work email and emailed me, asking me for my number so we could talk. Of course, I was shocked to see his name pop up in my email and immediately responded with my number, and not a minute went by before my phone rang with an out-of-town number. I simply grinned, picked up the phone, and said hello. As soon as I heard his voice, I was flooded with memories and nostalgia. We talked for hours, discussing all of our life events, failed marriages, new relationships, children, and tragedies. My boyfriend at the time, Paul, did not like the fact that he contacted me and told me immediately not to talk to him again, and convinced me that he was looking for something more. Another few years passed, and then once again out of the blue, he contacted me.

I was going through a rough time with Ben, and I was staying up late, reading a book in the living room, then once again out of nowhere, Carter texted me. I was thrilled. He was married and had kids and was starting to feel the midlife wiggle bug. It was really fun to connect with him again. We had not grown so different from each other. Yes, we were both adults and very different from our high school selves, but our ideals in life grew in the same direction. We talked about some of our similar dreams like owning a cabin in Alaska, living off the grid, producing all of our own food, foraging the forest, and living out life in the woods. We both talked about our troubles in life and found some comfort in each other. I asked him why he had contacted me, and he told me that throughout his life when he has trouble sleeping, he would picture my face to find peace. That did not answer my question, but it sure was nice to hear that there was someone out there thinking of me at odd hours in the night.

We both knew that these idle talks were just that, idle, to fill a space, to take up some time otherwise spent being lonely or sad. We knew that nothing would come of it, but it was a nice reprieve from everyday life. We chatted for about a week, and then I think his wife found out and put the kibosh on that. That was about two years ago.

This November after Ben had left, after Thanksgiving when I was feeling pretty blue and alone, having just spent my first holiday without my children and a partner, I received another unexpected text from Carter. This time he got right to the point. He was getting a divorce and needed advice from someone who had gone through a divorce. Although empathetic for his situation, I was not really that shocked.

I had been out of my relationship with Ben for about four months, and so timing was perfect for us to casually catch up. Once again, we reminisced about our old times, but this time, I had brought out my old journals from high school. I would read to him some of the entries that I had made, and each one brought back a new memory that we relished. Talking to him took my mind off my current misery, and I started to find some form of joy again. We started talking every day, and we laughed so hard with each other. We sent pictures to each other of our animals, our kids, our hobbies, and our lives. We talked about seeing each other at some point in the future, and wouldn't you know, that opportunity came around sooner than expected.

It just so happened that my favorite artist was having a show in Denver where he lived. He had gone to see the exhibit and told me about it. Then, like the universe was speaking to me, my cousin called me and told me she had bought me tickets to the exhibit because she knew my freakish passion for this artist.

A plan started to form. I was going to drive to Denver and get a hotel for two nights. I would incorporate a teaching opportunity within the exhibit and that way could go during the week. I booked a hotel right next to his work, and we planned to get together the evening I arrived. We were so excited, and for the next two weeks, we were giddy with the opportunity to see each other again. As we discussed it more and more, we both hinted at the fact that we not only wanted to catch up on our friendship but also possibly rekindle some romance as well.

The six-hour drive to the city was exhilarating. I listened to music, processed my eagerness to see my high school love again and the opportunity to see my favorite artist's work in person. What an awesome time this was going to be! I arrived around two o'clock in the afternoon, and he got off work at three o'clock so I had some time to settle my jitters and fix myself up. I was sitting on the couch when I heard his knock. I opened the door, and there he was, Carter, older, bearded, beer-bellied, and beaming! I immediately jumped into his arms, and we hugged with all the years dissipating through our embrace.

It felt so natural and so real, yet was still a bit awkward. There was a lot of anticipation for this moment, and I don't think that either of us knew what to do or say. Thank goodness, he had brought some beer! He poured us each a beer and sat down next to me. I just wanted to stare at him for a while, take it all in. I wanted to look at the man who had been the boy I had grown up with. I could see in his eyes that life had taken its toll. He looked tired and stressed, but I could also see the twinkle of his former self, the innocence and goofiness that I had fallen in love so many years ago. I could see the smile in his eyes as he was staring at me. I had aged well. I looked way better than I ever did in high school. I had worked very hard on staying healthy and looking great.

We settled in, got comfortable, and started talking. We talked about everything, we laughed, we held hands, and we leaned on each other. The more we talked, the closer we got until I was laying my head on his shoulder and he was caressing my hand. This part is hard to write about because at the time he was still married. He had assured me that the process of divorce was in the works and that there was no going back. After listening to him explain his current situation, I was confident in trusting him. So the afternoon turned to evening, and we got closer and closer until we eventually made it to the bed and made love.

I made love to a completely different person than the one who had taken my virginity. This time we were adults, we knew what we were doing, and we were both very eager to be intimately connected again.

Not to be rude, but it was less than I anticipated, and it was over before I knew it. I was not disappointed because it was the connection that I had craved. As soon as we had the obligatory cuddle, we both got up, made some funny one-liners to clear the awkward air, and returned to our clothing. I thought we would sit down again and maybe just sit in silence for a while and return to our storytelling, but to my surprise, he headed for the door, explaining that he had to get home to his daughter. I was not expecting that. I quickly stumbled over my words to assure him that I had anticipated this quick departure and that I was just fine with it. We took a picture of us, and he was out the door. It was only 6:00 p.m.

Here I was, all alone again, starving for attention, light-headed from the emotions and the sex and the beer. I didn't know who I was or what I was doing. So, I resorted to my automatic self, put on my headphones, and grabbed a cigarette. I went outside and just sat in the parking lot, listening to music and smoking, reeling from what had just happened. Was I okay with this? Is this what I expected? Did I feel good? The answers to all of these were hell no! I felt like shit. I started to cry. I felt once again like I was a second choice, not worth staying the night with, not worth the fight. I contemplated driving home that night, but I knew I had had too many beers and I did not want to miss the art exhibit. So I just listened to my music louder, had a dance party in the stairwell, and smoked and drank more until I finally lay down and passed out.

The next morning, I was up and running on the treadmill in the hotel gym. I was pumping myself back up, trying to feel my energy, the lightness I had felt on the drive there, trying to feel empowered, and it started working until I started thinking about last night's events. But I pushed those thoughts aside and stared at myself in the mirror while I was jogging. I pushed myself to rid myself of all negative thoughts. Luckily I had to teach a class via Zoom that day, so after my jog and a shower, I started working.

I remained focused on my task through the day, but when my work was completed and I was out of things to keep me busy, I started to think about what happened last night and our plans for tonight. Of course, that morning, Carter had texted, and throughout the day we texted and made plans for a similar evening. I could not really face myself because I was ashamed. I talked myself into thinking that everything was fine and that I wanted to see him again and repeat last night. When all I really wanted was to feel loved and happy, I wanted the joy to return, so I simply decided to ignore my other thoughts and fuck it!

To pass the time in between work and when Carter would arrive, I went for a swim in the hotel pool, then to the liquor store to buy some beer. I cleaned myself up and sat down on the couch with a book waiting for the anticipated knock on the door. And there it was at exactly three o'clock. He was there, and I opened the door to another grinning Carter. That evening went exactly like the previous, but it was the last night I was there, so our conversations went a little deeper into our past. I had learned about some tragedies he and his soon-to-be ex-wife had experienced, and I came to understand his view on divorce, family, and the future.

Just like clockwork, after a few beers and squishing our bodies together, we ended up in bed again. Nothing different, pretty much a repeat. Done, cuddle, clothes, door. Then once again, he was gone, he left to go home to his family, and I was stuck in a hotel to waste away an evening. It felt eerily similar to when Ben had left and had gone back to his "family."

What the hell was I doing? Why was I letting myself be in this place again. Why was I being so nice to listen to someone talk about their terrible ex-wife and their horrible homelife, then leave me after fulfilling his sexual desires to go back to his "terrible wife"? Was I stupid or something?

I wanted to believe everything he told me, and I wanted to believe everything I told him, but I was starting to feel used. Carter had always truly loved me, he had proven that time and time again, but this time I think he was just a lost man trying to find his joy and get his rocks off in the process. I was simply a rental Porsche for this man's midlife crisis.

That night as I lay in bed, Carter texted me and asked if I would stay one more night. Of course, that felt so good to be wanted that I agreed and booked another night at the hotel.

I do not need to explain the third day and night as it was the exact same pathetic shit.

When I finally left the city and was driving the six hours back home, I felt revitalized. I had been depleted, then loved, then left, then loved and left again. But I was on my way home, and I had some fleeting thought that I was possibly desired. As I sang to my music and cleared my head, I got a text. Surprisingly it was not Carter, but Ben. He texted to tell me that he loved me and missed me and wanted to come home but, of course, couldn't. He said that I was his soul mate and true love. What the hell? What was I supposed to do with that information? Do I say "thank you, but you left, so go fuck yourself"? Or do I say "thank you, I love you too, and want you back and go fuck yourself"? I had no idea how to react, but that didn't matter because before I could text a reaction, I got a text from Sam (next chapter) saying that he was craving me and asked if I would hang out with him soon. What the *hell* was going on? All of my exes were blowing up my phone, regretting the loss of me in their life, yet not willing to make any changes. They all just wanted to be with me when it was convenient to them, but not put any effort or work into it?

All of this sent me reeling. I felt good and I felt wanted, but I felt so miserably alone and used. What was happening in my life? Well, I'll tell you, life was happening, and these events were all leading up to the big change.

When I got home, Carter and I continued talking, but something had changed with him. He told me that as soon as he came home last night to his family, his wife had noticed how happy he was, and she changed her mind about the divorce. He explained it by saying that she was resolved on getting a divorce until he had finally said that he wanted a divorce too and stopped being depressed but started being happy. In his words, she missed him pining for her and begging for her to change her mind. As soon as she saw the end was really happening, she insisted they go to marriage counseling and try to make the marriage work.

Once again, I was the nice girl, and I supported his decision. I told him to fight for his family, that divorce sucks, and that if he still loves his wife then he should try to make it work. He was confused. He continued to text me and call me and be confused about his future and his feelings. He would go from dreaming about a future with me to needing to make things work with his wife.

One night when Carter and I were on the phone and I could tell he had been drinking a lot, I heard a woman's voice scream, "Is that Dory? Are you talking to her on the phone." Carter quickly said, "I gotta go," and hung up. The next morning, I wake up to a Facebook message from none other than Carter's wife.

My adrenaline popped, and I devoured the message. She expressed her disgust for my relationship with her husband and how it was ghastly inappropriate. She also explained that Carter had been lying to her and most likely lying to me. She said that Carter had agreed to go to marriage counseling and asked me to quit all communication with him while he was in the family home. She then wished me a happy holiday season. Her message was firm, to the point, and honestly very respectable. I wrote back that I respected her, her daughter, and Carter, that I would respect her wishes and not contact Carter when he was home.

I discussed all of this with Carter, and things got more and more complicated. I do not want to bore you with more details, so let's just jump to the last juicy part. Carter never did cease his contact with me, but instead, we chatted while he was at work or in the car, never at home. But then I got another FB message from Carter's wife, and she told me Carter had come clean about sleeping with me, and that she and I were both victims in this situation. She also told me that Carter had told her that he did not love me. He was just filling a void, and I was an escape from his reality. I apologized for my part in this and told her my understanding of their relationship. I told her that I would cease all communication with Carter and advised her not to give up on him and that their family was worth the fight. We both appreciated the candid conversation, and that was that. So I thought.

Carter emailed me a day later, saying that his wife hacked his phone and read all of our conversations and that she knew everything and that nothing had changed in his mind about me and our future, but that he had to go to marriage counseling and that he had to search his heart and soul.

The next email I got from his was "Don't forget about me."

Then I got another one about a week later saying, "When can you zoom / FaceTime I am going through a bit."

I told him when I was available, and the following evening we were talking through FaceTime. He told me that his stepmother had passed away, that he had gone to Florida to be with her, and when he returned from the depressing situation with his father, he returned to a depressing situation with his wife. He was sad, lost, and realizing his truth. I told him that I was fine, that I was happy, and to go live his life and fix his family. We ended that call, and I have not spoken to him since.

Back down to the bottom of the ravine I lay, face planted in the dirt, with just a mess of broken relationships all around me. What was I going to do, how was I going to be okay?

Well, I did what any normal person would do. I looked on Pinterest for more motivational quotes! I put back my "You are worth it" poster on my bathroom mirror. I made a vision board. I started running more. I started meditating, and I did *not* contact him. I felt used. I felt angry with myself for letting him use me.

I had to stand up for myself and prove my worth and what better time to do that than right now! I am worth it, damn it! I am worth it! I am worth it. I know I am. I am a catch! I have two master's degrees, I have a long-standing career and am well-known in the community as being a great leader and teacher. I have a house, a car, two kids with excellent grades, and a work ethic you cannot teach! I have two dogs who love me unconditionally, and I have fifteen chickens, and four ducks. I have a stream running through my yard. I know how to check my oil and change my tires. I am in excellent shape. I look like I am thirty but am forty-three. I am funny and can laugh at myself. Yeah, I am a catch, but here I am in this situation where no one is fighting for me.

So this is what I learned. I have to *fight for myself!* I have to show myself that I am worth it. After all, I am guaranteed to spend the rest of my life with me, so I better start learning to love that person!

But how do I start proving to myself that when for countless years I have been telling myself the exact opposite. How do I apologize for never standing up for myself? How do I choose myself first? Simple. I just do. I am worth it, I am worth the fight. If I have to tell myself that every day to prove it, then that is what I will do. I have to quit my old habits and start my new ones! So, thanks to Carter, I am now doing that. What a lesson!

Here is my letter to Carter.

Dear Carter,

Where do I start? At the beginning? In the middle? Or the end? Definitely a lot of stories in all of those parts, but the best story is the love that we shared. I loved it when you would sneak out of your house, hitchhike to my house at midnight, and come to my bedroom window. I thought it was so romantic, and my heart felt full. Looking back through my journals, I fell in love with us, our love, and our innocence all over again. Once, I wrote, "Carter told me that he loved me so much that if he could, he would rip out his heart and give it to me, that must be true love." Aweeee, so sweet, gruesome, to the point, and totally awesome!.

Thank you for that! Thank you for showing me how to love with no fear. How to let myself be loved without fear. How to enjoy the moments and express every feeling you have. You were an amazing high school boyfriend, and I could never ask for more.

Our most recent experience, on the other hand, was very sad. I know you wanted to be loved again and rekindle a feeling of being loved. But all we did was hurt ourselves and your family. In the end you made me feel worthless. Those nights in the hotel, you made me feel like a whore. But I also made myself a whore. I wanted so badly to be in love and feel appreciated and worth your love that I forgot to love myself. For that, I am sorry. But I am also very grateful. Because without these moments, I would have never found my worth.

You see, as I picked myself up again off the dirt floor from which you threw me, I found something. I found a voice, almost silent, but it was there. It was telling me that I was worth more than how I had been treated. That I could be loved and fought for, but in order for someone else to do that, I had to do it first. I had to stand up for myself, and I did not do that with you. So thank you for helping me to find my self-worth through your disposal of me. It is like I had to have someone knock me over in order to find my balance. And guess what, I am finding it!

I hope your family can heal and move forward. I hope you and your wife can once again find the love that once was a flame. I hope your daughter can learn how to fight for what is right and work through relationships even when the worst happens. I hope you find all the happiness with yourself and your family. Midlife crises are for the weak, and, Carter, you are not weak. Stay the course, fight the good fight, and love yourself.

Love, me

I will smile through it all
and I will dance until I fall,
so don't worry about me
and I won't worry about you.
("Meet Again," LP Giobbi)

CHAPTER 5

Learn to Say No

Breathe and remember who the fuck you are.
—Anonymous

As you can probably see from reading about my past, I have a hard time saying no. I was brought up by an empathetic mother who always taught me to put others' feelings first. Don't get me wrong, I am so thankful that I have a kind heart full of sympathy and empathy, but I was never taught to stand up for myself, to be picky, to tend to my own feelings instead of others. So as an adult, the hardest lesson I have had to learn on my own is how to say no. Let me just say, this action is a work in progress. I have had to change my entire process of thinking, accepting, receiving, and giving. The simple act of saying no used to fill me with such guilt that I could not stomach it. I would rather teach every single day, weekends, and summers too than say no to a disappointed boss. But, through a very strange relationship, I have learned that saying no is extremely important, healthy, and sometimes critical.

The summer after Ben left me, I was living in a tunnel of sadness with a lonely heart. After about two weeks of this feeling being my only constant, I decided that if I did not go do something outside for fun, I would slowly become a piece of mold in this damp dark world I was living in. So considering that I had not eaten substantial food in weeks and had lost a good amount of weight, I decided that it was time to put on my swimsuit and take my dogs to the river. I went to one of my favorite spots that was usually pretty empty. I was really hoping no one would be there, but to my dismay, there was a man sitting shirtless on the shore. I did not want to turn around and disappoint my dogs who were lunging toward the water, so I continued on my way. I gave a friendly wave to the man and found a spot to lay out my towel and my things. I immediately put on my headphones as a "don't talk to me" signal and watched my dogs lap up the sun and swim in the water. After laying in the sun for a while, I started to get pretty hot, so I decided to go for a dip. I took off my headphones and walked to the water. Of course, as soon as my "don't talk to me" signal was no longer blinking, the man on the beach went full-fledged into a conversation. Didn't he know, this was the reason I did not leave my depressing tunnel of sadness! Obviously, I did not feel like talking to anyone. I could not fake being happy, and I did not want to be mean to people. I just wanted to be alone!

However, since I could tell that he was a lot younger than me, some of my worries left because I really did not care about impressing him or even being nice. But to my surprise, the conversation actually felt kind of good. I remembered that I was still human and could answer normal casual questions, like "Are you from here?" "What do you do for fun?" It was actually simple to just talk to someone I did not know and did not give a fuck about.

I eventually started to get chilly in the crisp river water and returned to my beach towel. I was relieved when I saw the man put on his shirt and his shoes and get ready to leave. Finally I would have the beach to myself. However, before he left, he turned around and asked if I wanted to go for a hike sometime. I considered this and thought about it and then said, "A hike would be just perfect." Fuck it, right? I was newly single, and it can't hurt to just be outside and talk with someone. So we made plans to meet up the next afternoon for a hike.

I really did not know what I was thinking about accepting this invitation, but screw it, I was not going to sit in my house again feeling sorry for myself. The nice thing was that I was not attracted to this man whatsoever. He was really young, had pockmarks on his face and back from either bad acne as a teenager or something else, and he had really thin hair. He also had really intense eyes, and there was just something about them that made him appear a bit off. But what the hell, I was going for a hike, and I was not going to be alone.

The next day, we met up at the trailhead and set off on our hike. I had brought my dogs with me (of course) and was glad to see that Sam was very good with them. We talked about simple stuff to get to know each other. I found out a bit about his family, what brought him to our town, what he did for a living, and, you know, basic stuff. The hike was, to my surprise, actually really fun. I found Sam to be an intelligent, educated, and very interesting man with a different perspective. We hiked for a long time and then returned to our cars and gave each other a friendly hug to say goodbye. Reflecting on the experience that night, I smiled for the first time in what seemed like ages, because I realized that I had spent two hours of that day *not* thinking about Ben.

We followed up with texts and more meetups to walk the river trail, hike, or go to dinner. After about the first two dates with him, I started figuring out that he was a very unique person and, actually, a bit odd. I could not really figure him out. There was just something peculiar about him. But I found his company to be better than no company. Plus, he was an amazing listener.

On one of our river walks, we bumped into one of my dear friends, Luisa, who was on the trail a lot because she was a rafting photographer. I introduced the two of them, and I promised Luisa to catch up with her later that afternoon. We continued on our way and even jumped in the river for a swim. Once our walk was over, I got on my bike and met back up with Luisa as promised. I parked my bike when I found her and walked over to where she was taking pictures. Luisa immediately asked me where I had met Sam. I told her about the river encounter, and she then told me a strange story.

For over a year now, she and her husband saw Sam a lot. They saw him either on the river trail or at the coffee shop that they lived near. They thought it was curious that on their way home from the coffee shop early in the morning they would see him running, and then at night when they were out for a walk they saw him running again. They came to the conclusion that he was homeless and was either at the coffee shop or on the river trail because he had nowhere else to be. They also got a really strange feeling from him and did not trust him. As a matter of fact, her husband had told her to stay away from him if she ever found herself in his presence alone. She explained how she just felt something very disturbing about him.

I was surprised to hear about the homeless part but not about the strange vibe. I had felt the same thing. However, I assured her that he was not homeless and that I had seen where he lived (which to my dismay was pretty awful) but that I would take her advice of caution into consideration.

Sam and I continued to text and meet up casually, and eventually we planned a camping trip. It's not that I did not take Luisa's advice seriously; it's just that I am an adult woman and I can make my own decisions.

Okay, I have to do this. I do not want to get into this, as it is very private and disturbing, but the reason I knew where he lived was because I had gone there after our dinner out and we had sex. But wait, it was not just sex. It was the craziest, dirtiest, naughtiest, strangest, disturbing, thrilling, unusual sex that I have ever had. He did things to my body I did not know was possible. He made me feel like I was a virgin. It was nuts, and I was not sure if I liked it. It was definitely out of my comfort zone, but there was something about it that made me think about doing it again.

But I digress. Okay, so one night, my friend Amy invited Luisa and me over to her house to celebrate her independence. Her roommate Jody had just moved out, and Amy was now in the position to finally have her boyfriend move in with her. We celebrated with wine, cheese, and the normal girlie foodie crap that they loved. Amy asked how I was doing without Ben, and Luisa blurted out that I was kind of dating this weirdo named Sam. I then proceeded to tell Amy all about Sam and our planned camping trip. Luisa did not like this at all. She was scared for me. Amy knew better than to be nervous for me because she knew I was a pretty independent woman. So she asked to see a picture of Sam. I did not have any pictures of him, but I did have his Facebook profile. So I pulled that up and showed it to her. And when she took my phone to look at the picture, a look of utter disgust came over her face.

Amy recognized Sam. She not only recognized him but also she knew exactly who he was. He was Jody's (ex-roommate) ex-boyfriend. He was the reason that Jody moved out of state. He had destroyed Jody's mental health. According to Amy, Sam had made Jody's life a living hell. He stalked her and showed up at their house uninvited. He consumed her and made her do things she was uncomfortable with. He threatened suicide when she broke up with him and ended up going to some mental institute after that episode. *Yeah!* Go figure, the first guy I meet after Ben is actually a crazy dude!

I promised my two friends before I left that I would not continue a relationship with him and would cancel my camping trip. Immediately after leaving Amy's house, I texted Sam and just simply said, "WTF. I told you I was going to Amy's house and all along you knew exactly who Amy was! She was your ex-girlfriend's roommate." He promptly responded and apologized. He said that he was too nervous to bring it up and that I should not believe anything that was said about him and that Jody was the crazy one. How did he know they were going to say weird shit about him? I felt my anger building, and at the same time, I was nervous too. What if this guy is totally crazy? What if I tell him I don't want to see him anymore and he goes all stalker crazy on me? I did not want to make any decisions that night, so I just told him that I was upset and that I just needed time to think.

The next day, the first email I sent was to my therapist. I needed to update her on Ben, process that whole thing with her, and then ask her how to kindly tell a possibly unstable person that you are not interested in them.

Thankfully my therapist had an opening that very evening. When I got home that night, I had a phone session with her. We spent the majority of the hour talking about my recent breakup from Ben. She gave me direct orders not to date for an entire year! Ha! Then I told her about my recent predicament. After I explained who Sam was and what was going on, she replied with some interesting questions. Does he mountain bike and run every day? Why, yes, he does. Does he do work as a computer coder as a living? Why, yes, he does, how did she know that? She very calmly said, "Dory, I know who this is, and he is very unstable. I cannot give you any details due to client confidentiality, but I am allowed to tell you as a safety precaution that he has been a patient in many mental institutes." Wow! Really? This was really happening? Good thing, I was not too attached to him. She advised me to quickly text him that I no longer wanted to see him and to no longer contact me.

So that was that. Easy. I would just text him and tell him that I could not see him again and have a great life. But... Yes, there is a but, after thinking about everything she told me, I was kind of feeling intrigued. I mean, I love strange people! But who was I kidding. I was not attracted to him, I knew I did not want him as a boyfriend, I just wanted to have a hiking/camping partner, but I could not lead him on, so it was what it was. I had to tell him goodbye.

So that night, I sent him a text telling him I could not see him anymore. As I was waiting for a text back, the phone rang instead. He wanted to talk it out on the phone. I told him a few things, nothing really in detail, and just said that it was not going to work and that I was too old for him anyways and thanks for the good times. He tried to convince me over and over to continue seeing him, but I stuck to my guns and just said no. Once I hung up, I blocked his number. Done.

Nope! Five minutes later, I got a text from an unknown number, and lo and behold, it was Sam. I couldn't believe it, he texted me through a different number! I almost started laughing because it was so nuts. But instead, I just blocked that number, and then five minutes later, he texted me through another number! Holy shit, this is some really creepy shit! I'm thrilled yet scared, but thrilled! In that third text, he informed me that there are apps where you can get a new phone number to text someone who has blocked you! Well, of course, there is, our world is crazy! He said that if I really wanted him to stop contacting me, then all I had to say was "Don't contact me" Well, gee, I thought that was what I was saying when I told him that I could not see him anymore and then blocked his number, but I guess it was not enough, so I did as he instructed and wrote, "Please do not contact me again."

I felt terrible! I felt like a bad person. I had never been that straightforward to someone, especially someone who had some serious issues and needed help. I was a helper!

I lasted three days without contacting him and without hearing from him, then I broke down. I texted him a simple "I hope you are doing well" text and had an immediate response from him. Well, damn it, I did it! I opened up the box I had just shut, and well, this time, it was not so easy to close. Sam and I picked back up where we had left off, and we started by having a long conversation about his past and what others were saying about him.

According to Sam, he had had a rough childhood. His parents "drugged" him against his will and took him to specialists all the time. They had him seen by psychiatrists, and he was diagnosed with schizophrenia when he was younger. He had had several experiences being hospitalized in mental institutes for up to ten days. He said that he was always drugged without consent and that he felt that the staff was trying to hurt him. He had delusions that people were attacking him and that if he did not do or say certain things, the shape-shifters would place harm on him and those he loved.

He was fascinating! He was not scary in the slightest bit. He was kind. He listened to me and gave me interesting advice. He spoke of manifesting his future and visualizing what he wanted in life. He also told me about his job, or lack thereof. He did not have a job, he actually received disability and food stamps, and every day he either ran, mountain biked, or worked on his websites (which were simple websites with photos he took and a donation page to help him in his struggle). He actually felt that society owed him money for the injustice he had been put through by the psychiatric system.

We did end up going camping. We went camping twice. We had a wonderful time. We hiked, talked about existential shit. I told him about all of my past relationships and a lot about Ben. He listened, he did not judge me, and he just let me talk. Out of all of my relationships, he was actually kind of the sanest one. I know, weird, but hear me out. He did not abuse me (like Paul), he did not have a secret family that he hid from me (like Ben), and he did not lie to me, use me for a midlife crisis sexcapade, then ghost me (like Carter). He told it like it was. He knew he was different, he knew who I was, and he was Sam that's all, just Sam.

But there was a problem. I knew that what I was doing was wrong. I knew that I did not want a relationship with him and that even though I was enjoying our hikes, camping trips, talks, and sex, I was not in love with him and had no intention of having a future with him. He, on the other hand, wanted a relationship with me, a real relationship. He had been so honest and vulnerable to me, I wanted to give him the same respect. So I eventually had to come clean and tell him that I was not interested in pursuing a relationship with him. But this time, I told him that it was *not* because what anyone else said or told me. It was because I knew that this was not going anywhere, that our age difference, our different ideals of career, and the really strange sex were just not something I wanted in a partner. He fought this pretty hard, but in the end, he totally respected my decision and stopped texting every day. He just texted once a week. :)

I was okay with that because I wanted him to know that I did not hate him, but I just could not have a relationship with him. I also wanted to be there for him if he had a breakdown and was in trouble. We kept it simple, just checking in with each other to say hey, and hope you are doing well. After a few weeks of this consistent weekly check-in, I thought it was odd when I did not hear from him for about two weeks in a row. I started to get a sense that something was wrong. I never saw his car parked by his house (which was downtown, so I drove past it every day), he did not respond to my texts, and that was just odd. I started to get worried. I texted him expressing my concern and worry for him, but with the same outcome, silence. A few days went by, and then I just knew something was wrong. I called the local hospital to see if he was there, nope, then I called the mental health facility institute in town. They could neither confirm nor deny if he had been admitted. So to save myself from thinking the worst, I looked up his mom on Facebook and reached out.

Before I got a response from her, Sam texted me. He told me that I was really "in tune with his spirit" because he had, in fact, been gone. He had driven himself to the hospital to be admitted for his panic attacks, and they took him to a mental institute out of town. He stayed there for ten days and then temporarily moved back in with his parents. When he contacted me, he was still there with his parents. He had told me that losing me brought on some very evil spirits into his life, and he thought he was getting attacked and, worse, that his thoughts were causing evil in my life.

Oh, Sam, what a struggle he goes through on a daily basis. I feel empathy for his situation. Because it is truly his struggle and he is really alone. But, he was amazing and I learned a lot from him, and the most important thing I learned from him was when to say *no*.

My time with Sam was well spent. After meeting him and having the experiences I had with him, I really reflected on some of my choices and my unquenchable thirst for approval from others.

Sam helped confirm that my decision of stepping away from the administration program was the right thing to do for me. He also helped me reflect on my financial situation. At the time I met Sam, I had five life insurance policies on me. Why did I ever think I needed five life insurances?? I just could never say no to those people who came into our school convincing me I needed more policies for this and that! I have since then cancelled them because I realize how stupid it is to have something that costs me money just because I could not let the salesperson down!

Since Sam, I have been able to say no the first time instead of having to back out on plans. My cousin literally called me the bailer because I bail on everything! I am too scared to say no when I am invited to something because I am afraid I will hurt their feelings. Instead, I say yes to appease them, then I cancel at the last minute. This has been my MO for years! So much so that my sister and mother are literally shocked when now I say no to their invite instead of "Yeah, that sounds fun," then calling right before the event and give them some lame excuse. Now I just say no, thank you, but thank you for the invite. *It* is soooooo freeing. It is a whole new world when I participate in things I actually want to and have the guts to say no when I don't want to do something. I have so much more respect for myself, and here is the thing, so do others!

I am finally okay with accepting the fact that I may hurt someone's feelings by saying no to their invitation, but since I am being honest, they are not hurt because they know that I am just being me. I am standing up for myself by myself and it feels amazing, and I have Sam to thank for that.

This my letter to Sam.

Dear Sam,

Swimming with you in the river made me feel alive during a time that I thought I had stopped living. Going on hikes with you, camping with you, and just hanging out with you was enlightening and empowering. You let me talk about my ex, the pain I had felt from that, and what I was learning about myself. You never judged me, but always had something very kind to say about the experience, or suggest a new way to look at the situation.

I want to thank you for the time you shared yourself with me. Even though it was not long, it was absolutely crucial to my self-growth. You helped me rethink my choices, my future, and how I needed to be living in the present. You opened my eyes to new ways of saying things with intention. I had never thought about the power of words, and when you talked about the phrase "let it go" and how you preferred to say "let it flow" because it was more positive, I listened.

I know that hearing the things that some people said about you was hard, but it helped me to decide to not listen to them but to make my own choices. And I am glad I chose to spend time with you. Thank you for the wonderful lessons you have shared with me. I wish you peace and joy.

Love, me

This is a song for those who lost their hope a
    long, long time ago
I know someday that you will find it somehow
Because you are not too old to accomplish your
    goals.
And all the answers are within your soul
It's up to you, you gotta figure it out…
You better take some action right now
Oh, yes, because there's nothing in the world that
    you can't get
So don't fill your life with confusion and regret
You better take some chances right now.
                    ("Courage to Grow," Rebelution)

CHAPTER 6

Redemption

Number 1 rule: Fuck what they think.

Whenever I see the word *redemption*, I think of the song by Bob Marley. I guess this book is my redemption song, and this year is my redemption year. I know that all of us go through struggles. Some people hide it really well, others not. I like to think of people like ducks. We are all swimming through the raging river to get to the other side. On top of the water, the duck looks so in control and graceful, like swimming against the current is so very easy, but under the water, the part we do not see, those little duck feet are ruthlessly paddling through the turbulent water just to survive. Everyone has a struggle, and we are all just trying to get to the other side without having our struggle be too obvious, or take over.

For once I want to get out of the turbulent river, find a nice calm pool, and float in the water with peace, joy, and freedom! I am taking charge of my life, I am making choices that I want, and I am seeing things for what they are. I am being grateful to all of my exes and the hard lessons I have learned through the experience. And now, I am moving forward. And that is what *my* redemption is all about. Taking charge of my life and loving it!

My path to redemption:

Step 1: *Fall in love!*

I am falling in love. Well, in reality, I have fallen in love, and she is perfect. No, I have not switched teams, which, of course, I have no problem with, but I have just fallen in love with myself. Yep! You heard it here first. *I am in love!* All of these relationships and the lessons I've learned have brought me to this perfect place in my life where I finally love myself. I am embracing all of my imperfections and the qualities that I used to be ashamed of or thought I had to hide. I am not trying to prove something to anyone else. I am only trying to prove to myself that this is my life and I deserve to enjoy it! I have the choice to live the life that unfolds before me or live the life that I make. And for once, I am choosing to live the life that I make, the life of my dreams.

I started this journey of loving myself this past year. Being in the depths of the deepest darkest canyon was painful and lonely, but it was perfect because I was there with myself and the only person I could depend on was myself. I had to figure out how to make the trek out of that damn canyon and climb out. But it was not easy. I had to pick my face up off the dirty floor, slowly lift my body up, and brush myself up. I had to pick up all the pieces of me that were broken and then slowly claw my way out of that canyon. Sometimes I would find a solitude tree root sticking out to give me a boost. Sometimes I could grab on to that root and hold on to it with all my strength, only to find myself falling again. Sometimes I would make it past that root and find a ledge to crawl up on and sit and rest. From there I could see how far I had climbed, but also see how far I had to go. It was there on that ledge that I started embracing my strength and my ability to not only reach the top but also to actually keep climbing until I climbed up the highest rocks and balanced on the tip of the rock with my feet firmly planted. And that is *exactly* what I am doing. Learning to forgive myself, accept myself, know my own self-worth, and say no has given me the ability to redeem myself and create the life I want. I can do anything now because I know that I found the person I want to spend the rest of my life with! And that person's name is Dory. Of course, I still want a partner to spend my life with, but I know that is coming soon, but this time is for me, for myself, to love myself and make dreams come true.

Step 2: *Find inspiration!*

One of the steps I took toward climbing out of my canyon was to start listening to myself even if my thoughts were angry. So I looked for inspiration on Pinterest. Of course, I found sappy quotes and sad quotes, but that was not what I was looking for. I kept searching until I at last found the quote that made me smile. "Number 1 rule, fuck what they think." Ahhhhh, yes, this hit home. I was pissed, and I did not give a shit about letting everyone see that and know it. I needed to just be me and let myself go. So I found every "fuck it" type of quote I could find and put them everywhere! I wrote them on my mirrors, then I printed them out and taped them to my treadmill, my walls, and my dashboard on my car. I posted pictures of me on Facebook claiming that my new motto was "fuck it." Then something happened. Just by embracing the idea that I did not have to care about what other people thought, I started just doing whatever the fuck I wanted. I read a wonderful book by Mark Manson called *The Subtle Art of Not Giving a Fuck*, and I really started to weed through the items in my life that were not important and started focusing on what was important to *me*.

This became my life. I just started being me and not really caring about petty shit that used to claim so much of my time and energy. One very good example of this was in the parking lot of a grocery store. I was looking for a spot to park, and I had never been that picky, so I was just casually looking around. I saw that someone in front of me was backing out of their space, and I was right in line to take their space. Well, when they left, I noticed another car was waiting on the other side to drive forward so their car would be facing forward for an easy exit. I had already started pulling into the spot and then realized what was happening,

Here is my inner dialogue:

Normal Dory: "Oh my goodness, how rude of me, I did not see them. By all means, they should have this spot. I mean, they have a spot that they are in right now, and they could easily just stay there, but they should have this one too, because then they will be able to leave easier when they are done grocery shopping. I was silly to think that this was a spot for me."

"Don't give a fuck" Dory: "Ummm, hold on a second, I was here waiting patiently for this spot, and I also would like to park so I can get in and out of the grocery store and continue my day. Take the spot, Dory. It's perfect, right there in front of you, it's big enough, and these other people can just stay in the spot they already have."

Normal Dory: "But what if they get mad. I would much rather see a friendly hand wave than a middle finger. I do not want to be rude. They should have it, they deserve it more."

"Don't give a fuck" Dory: "Who the hell cares if they get mad. It is not like you called them a bad name or said something rude. You simply found a parking spot, waited patiently, and now have the chance to just park. Get the hell over it and park already. If they get mad at you, let them and see if it changes your life."

So I put my car back into first gear and just stared back at them. Eventually they reversed, and I pulled in and parked. And to my amazement, they did not yell at me, and they did not flip me off. They just smiled, and we both went along with our grocery shopping business. It was amazing! I realized then that I can just start living my life and not the life I perceive others think I should live. I actually can choose what I should really care about and what to not give a fuck about! I don't want to be rude or unkind, but I do not have to put up with anything that I don't want to. This freedom has been amazing!

I have been able to really focus on what I care about and what I simply do not. Another time this came up was with a Facebook encounter. I had seen this one guy's posts for a long time and was intrigued about his musical talent, so one night I decided to message him (this was during my very strong *fuck it* stage, so beware). Anyways, it was a simple DM saying something about how I liked his posts and was just reaching out to say hello. He wrote back and said something to the effects of not using Facebook too much except for music, and then he talked a lot about what he does and his music. I responded cynically and said, "Yeah, fuck Facebook, right?" And then, ten minutes later, he finally responded and said, "I guess," and then nothing else for the rest of the night and for that matter ever again. I started trying to process what happened. What did I do wrong? Did I offend him with my foul language? Then I started to worry about it and thought about sending an apology. Should I tell him that I am not really a rude or vulgar person, but then I asked myself, do I really care what he thinks of me? I have never met him, he wrote way too much about himself and never said anything, like, what do you do? My final answer? No! I did not care, I said what I wanted to say. If he didn't like it, who the fuck cares? Not me!

Freeing, I tell you. This new light that I found was flashing like a strobe light, and I loved it! At the beginning, I did go a bit overboard with it. I started drinking way more than I should have and smoking whenever I wanted and just had the excuse of not caring what others thought. But I also knew that I didn't want to become a hate-filled selfish person that had bad habits and was rude. I had to find a balance. So I did some more searching and reading and listening to myself, and I focused a lot of my attention on thinking about what I really wanted in life. What was my dream life?

Step 3: *Do the research.*

I started reading more books and listening to podcasts that helped me find some focus. I printed out more Pinterest quotes and added them to the collection, this time with quotes like, "You are worth it," "Claim your worth," "The universe is amazing and so am I." Quotes with more of a positive message but still focusing on what I wanted to receive. I made a vision board with all the things I wanted and how I wanted to feel about myself. I had words on there about what I love about myself. I had pictures of a cabin in the woods, of a couple with an awesome camper van, and I had a picture of the beach and a museum that I want to go to. I had a picture of a wedding ring because I want to get married again. I had pictures of Wonder Woman, of horses, just anything I found inspiring and that I wanted in my life. I even had pictures of good-looking men.

Looking at this board every day has helped to remind myself that I can have everything my heart desires as long as I love myself (which I do now), and I am taking action to get that life.

Step 4: *Take action.*

Making the change in my life meant that I had to not only change the way I thought but also change my actions. If I wanted to be in shape, then I had to do the work. If I wanted to be a better friend, then I needed to commit to my friends. If I wanted a new car, then I had to figure out how to do that without breaking the bank.

This past year, I have been driving a piece-of-shit Subaru. Don't get me wrong, I love Subarus, but not this one. When Ben left, he took the new car we had bought together. We agreed that if I paid the monthly payments and insurance, then I would drive it and that he would finance it since I had just financed a new house. He had a truck fixed up for him by his stepfather who gifted it to him. He also had a car in his and his ex's name. I was in between cars and borrowing my sister's car. He traded in his financed car, and we got a small SUV we could fit our whole family in. His truck was kind of a gas beast, so I ended up buying him a commuter car, the piece-of-shit Subaru that is currently mine. So when he left me, he took the SUV and left me with his piece-of-shit Subaru. He sold his truck for a bunch of money and had a brand-new car. I was pissed, but I figured that I deserved it and that this was my luck. Within a week of driving it, I had to buy new tires, then get new brakes, then fix the clutch and more. I cleaned it, drove it, and accepted my fate to be a shitty Subaru owner. Well, the benefit was that it was paid for and I needed to save money. So Ben got a car and a huge car payment! I got a shitty car but no payment. I was able to save my money.

A bit more backstory so you can get the full effect of this moment. When I was twenty-four, I bought a white Toyota Tacoma by myself. I had my first real job, just got married, and I decided it was time to buy myself something that I wanted. I loved this truck, it was everything that I wanted and deserved. As soon as my ex-husband and I moved to California for his job, he convinced me to sell my truck so that he could buy a motorcycle because it would save us money on gas and insurance. He would let me drive his fifteen-year-old enormous Dodge pickup. Of course, I wanted to be nice, so before I even had a real chance to enjoy my first adult purchase, it was gone. Since that day, I have always said that I would get my Toyota Tacoma back. Well, it only took twenty years, but I did it.

So of course, when I made my vision board, I included my white Toyota Tacoma. I literally wrote down in my journal the exact truck I wanted, a white Toyota Tacoma TRD 4WD 2015 or older (I liked the old body style). Every time I saw one on the street, I would wave and just say, hey there, can't wait until I have mine. I just convinced myself it was going to happen.

A week ago, I found this beautiful truck on a website. It happened to be located at a used dealership in town. It was perfect, had everything I wanted, so I emailed the place and I set up a time to test drive it. It just so happens that the day before I was supposed to test drive the truck, my Subaru broke down. I had to have it towed and get the CV joint replaced. At the shop, they also found an oil leak and noted that it needed front brakes. I took this as a sign. I borrowed my mother's car, drove to the dealership, and took the Toyota out for a test drive.

The moment I got in the car, I knew that I would be driving home in it. I pulled out of the parking lot and said out loud to the car, "Hello there, beautiful, we are meant to be together! Let's make this work," and work it did! When I returned from my drive, I told the salesman that I wanted it. He responded by saying, "When I saw you get in that car, I swear I saw sparks fly" (weird thing to say about a car, flying sparks are never a good thing, but I knew what he was trying to say). Holy shit! He could feel the magic too! This was going to work, I knew it was. The next day, he called me and told me that they got me financed and the truck was mine and ready to be picked up. The white Toyota Tacoma TRD 4WD truck was mine!

I named her Yoda because I felt like I was using the force to get this truck and I must be strong with the force because it is sitting in my driveway. I had to put some money down, but I listed the POS Subaru for that same price and I sold it two days after listing it. I put that money right back in the bank, and it was like the deposit on my truck never happened.

I cannot make this up! This happened, and I am seeing it happen all around me. Because I finally believe in myself. Not only can I make things happen by taking action, but also by understanding my worth and knowing that I can make my dreams come true by just waking up and living my life the way I want to live it!

> There's still so much to discover.
> There's still a lot we don't know.
> Come alive.
> Give it up girl before you lose your mind.
> ("Come Alive," Chromeo)

CHAPTER 7

Music and Solo Dance Parties

*Something inside is hurting you, that's why
you need cigarettes or whiskey or music
turned so fucking loud you can't think.*

—Anonymous

I think that everyone should have a therapist. Well, only if they want, but I love mine and am grateful for all her help. I started working with my therapist when I had first met Paul. During one of my sessions, after Paul and I had broken up the first time, she told me something about dealing with pain that I will never forget. She told me that pain is like a child pulling on your pant leg, begging to be picked up. The child will not stop until you pay attention to it, pick it up, and embrace it. I always come back to this thought when I am in the middle of something emotionally painful. Pain is just one of those things that takes time to get through, but it also takes forgiveness. Time and forgiveness, however, are not the only solution to getting through pain. You also have to pay attention to it, give it center stage, focus on it, listen to it, and live in it. It will only go away when it is finished teaching you, and you will only learn from it if you pay attention. So even though many, including me, try to self-medicate or stay distracted, the pain will continue to be there until you give it what it needs. Feel the pain, acknowledge your loss, have a pity party, actually, have a dance party!

Now, I know that dancing may not be your thing. Maybe your thing is having a knitting competition or going hunting or kayaking in waterfalls or seeing how much chocolate you can eat before you get sick, but dancing is my thing. No, I am not a dancer, I never took ballet or jazz, and I am certainly not coordinated or rhythmic, but music speaks to me and I love to let it take over my body and mind. When I was younger, I loved going to dance clubs and just dancing all night long, As an adult, I looked forward to weddings so that I could have a dance floor to enjoy, but now I am too old to go to any dance clubs and I have not been to a wedding in years, so I have not been able to "go dancing" in so long.

The reason I like dancing and, for that matter, jogging, is because the music I play releases an energy inside of me. I lose my thoughts, and I get pulled into the rhythm. My body reacts to the music and just flows with the energy. It is a wonderful way for me to release energy and emote through the lyrics and the sound. For many years now, I have found my only dancing opportunities are when I jog, so naturally, dancing has been replaced by jogging. Well, that was true until I had my first dance party.

My first dance party took place on a Friday night soon after Ben had left. I had consumed plenty of wine or beer, I cannot remember which, or maybe it was Moscow mules. Anyways, I had a lot of alcohol and a bit of weed. I was feeling great. I was bored of watching TV, so I plugged my iPhone into my speaker and put on my running playlist. During this time, I was rediscovering music, and she (my music) and I were having a blast! She (music) introduced me to a lot of new music that has helped me cope through my pain. Anyways, the music started, and I was just standing there listening, and then I was singing and moving around. The song finished, and I started to move toward the couch to sit and just listen to music, but the next song started and this one was *reeaally* good. So, I figure, what the hell, no one is here and I cannot resist, so…looks like I am having a dance party!

It was one hell of a dance party. I let all my inhibitions go and let the music take over. I listened and danced, I sang, I sobbed, and I just absorbed all the emotions from the songs and let them take me for a ride. It was amazing!

This first dance party lasted three hours! Yeah, I know, a really long time, but each song had a different need, and I was releasing so much angst with each song. So I made this a routine. I had a dance party every Friday night that my children were at their dad's house (this is before he moved out of state). I was not ashamed of it. I embraced it and loved it. I looked forward to it, and unfortunately, I have not been able to have a dance party in a month because my kids are with me all the time. But now that I am thinking about it, I may have one this Friday and just put on my headphones and make my bedroom the club!

It may not be a dance party that you want, but whatever *you* need to do to release your pain, to feel your emotions, to emote your thoughts, to think, to be absorbed, and then to be exhausted and free, then do it. Who cares what anyone thinks, as long as it is a healthy outlet, just have fun and do it!

> Dancin' is what to do
> Dancin' is when I think of you
> Dancin' is what clears my soul
> Dancin' is what makes me whole.
>
> ("Dancin'," Aaron Smith)

CHAPTER 8

The Inevitable Fall

So I am finally here. I made it through the dark parts of my relationships and the heartache. I have found myself and my own self-adoration. I have taken action and changed my life. I have learned and applied my lessons to my daily life. But what if this feeling does not last.

I envision myself standing on top of the boulder that is on top of the mountain, miles above the deep canyon where my broken self once lay. I am doing a yoga pose with one foot planted firmly on the boulder and the other bent at the knee, ankle resting on the other leg's thigh. I am balanced, I am happy, and I *want a selfie*! I take out my phone and get the camera set up. I focus it on my smiling face when *beep, beep*, a text vibrates through my hand and chimes in my ear. Who could be texting me right now? Yep, you guessed it, no one other than the infamous Ben.

As soon as I see who the sender is, my whole balance is rocked, my rested leg unwraps and flies out to plant itself on the ground to gain balance, but as it swings out, I am tipped to the right, my arms grasping for something to hold on to, and then, I am falling, falling quickly back down to the depths of my depression canyon.

One text from Ben, and my whole world comes undone. Everything I worked through, every torture I overcame, every single step forward was for nothing because I was falling back down. But *no*! Not this time. I *will not* let this happen. I close my eyes, remember my love for myself, and then instead of falling, I am floating. Yes,

I am still heading down toward the bottom, but instead of crashing down, I am slowly floating down. I am just letting myself relax because I know I can.

Once I finally land softly on the ground, I just lay there for a while. I feel the pain of missing Ben. I start to cry, but the tears are soft and they feel good. I look up at the sky, and I know what I have to do this time.

I get up and just start walking. Instead of struggling and climbing out, clinging to any root of life, I am just walking. As I am doing this, I hear a familiar song in my head. It was a song that always made me think of Ben. A song that brought me to my knees in pain after Ben left, but this time, I just hum it and smile. I think about a happy memory of Ben. There were so many. I enjoy the song, and I do not shed a tear of sadness. These tears are tears of gratitude. I was thankful that I had all that wonderful time with Ben.

As I am walking, I look up at the canyon walls that grow steeply all around me. I notice a crevice in front of me. There is something there, something that looks like stairs made out of rocks. Holy shit! Are you kidding me? There have been stairs here the whole time? Why had I never noticed them before?

I head toward the stairs and start climbing up one at a time. They are actually really beautiful, and the view around me is amazing! As I am making my way up the stairs, I see some carvings in some of the steps. I try to make out what the carvings are, and some of them I see are just cool designs and others I see are words. On one particular stone, I see a word that draws me in. It says "BODD," my and Ben's initials. It reminds me of all the times we would write our initials in snow, on the trees, in the sand, and on our love notes. I smile at the memory, blow the rock a kiss, and keep stepping up.

The air is cool, but the sun is bright. It is a perfect spring day. My dogs are jumping up and down the stairs, darting off the path, peeing on everything and smiling at me! My dogs? Where the hell did they come from? I thought I was all alone! Turns out, I never was alone, I just thought I was. I am so grateful my dogs are with me. I love them so much! I call them over to me and give them loving, appreciative kisses.

I am surprised that I am not getting tired climbing up all of these stairs, but I am a bit hungry. I start to smell a familiar scent. A scent not a lot of people can determine, but I sure can since it is the scent of my favorite food. I smell…steamed artichokes. I do not see any steaming artichokes, but the smell takes me back to a memory of one of my birthdays. Paul and I went hiking for my birthday. It was a really intense steep hike. He was striding up like he was on a mission. At the top of the trail, overlooking the town, he pulled out a small pot, a jug of water, a portable camping stove, and artichokes. We sat there in the sunset eating artichokes. That memory is so beautiful, I can almost taste the artichokes now. Just having that thought gives me enough nourishment to continue climbing up these stairs.

I hear the rustle of leaves and the sound of my shoes stepping on the rocks below me. I love the sounds of nature. Then I hear something else familiar. It is pure innocent laughter, then voices, then more laughter. I could recognize those voices from anywhere. It is my children. And there, out of nowhere, are my kids. Man, they sure are tall! What amazing boys I have, and I am so grateful for their love. They come up to me, give me a great big hug, and then say, "Mom, these stairs are cool, but check out the escalator." Escalator? In the middle of nature? Well, duh, of course!

My kids love escalators. They think they are like this incredible scientific invention. Growing up in a small town makes big-city things like escalators and elevators a big deal. The first time I let them ride an escalator was in Denver. Their squeaky shrills of excitement from riding an escalator would make you think that they were on a fantastic ride at Disneyland. So of course, they would be the ones to find the escalators in the woods. And there, just like magic, escalators, an easy way to get up the mountain.

I step on the escalator and look all around me. I never realized that I had so much love and help available to me. I am finding that this time up I have been able to access what I have learned and make it to the top without too much trouble. I mean, yeah, thinking about my past and missing my lost loves hurt, but I know that these feelings are necessary and they will slowly fade.

As I am riding this escalator, I feel like I am floating. Everything disappears. It is quiet and serene. I can see that I am approaching the end of the escalator and that I am going to have to get off and once again stand on my own. I start talking through my thoughts about how I love myself and how I am ready for true love and I am ready to live my dream. I am scared, but at the same time, thrilled, because I know what to do when I fall. And I know who I can depend on and what makes me happy. I am scared that I am going to feel alone, but I know that I have my family, my animals, and myself for great company. Then, as I am preparing to step off the escalator, a hand reaches out to me. I don't recognize this hand, yet it is strangely familiar, almost like I have seen it in my dreams. I don't waste a second thinking about it. I reach forward and grab the extended hand. As I grasp this hand, I know. I know that I have found my true love. I know that I am holding the hand of my future.

FINALE

So through all of this jibber-jabber, what I am trying to tell you, dear readers, is that sometimes we have to look really deep inside of our souls. We have to take the time to get to know ourselves. We have to listen to ourselves and our surroundings to really figure out why things have happened in our past, and how we want to turn those experiences into knowledge. We need to start dreaming again and know that we have control over our reality, but if we do not know what we want, then we need to wait to find out. So here I am taking that time to really focus on what I want. But if I do not know, then maybe just stepping out of my comfort zone and trying something new may be just what I need.

This is my letter to myself

Dear Dory,

    I know that change is difficult, and I am so proud of you for taking charge of your life. I know that I have not been the nicest to you, and for that, I want to apologize. Dory, I am sorry. I am sorry that for every compliment I gave you, I also threw excuses at it to remove any notions of conceitedness or confidence. I am sorry that I never was just proud of you for being you, but that I made you prove yourself to others. I am sorry for always putting you down, for not giving you the credit you deserved. I always looked to other people to validate your worth instead of just telling you that I thought you were amazing!

I am sorry that I never told you that I loved you because you obviously did not know how incredible you are, and I should have been telling you that every day. I am sorry for making you think you were unlovable or unworthy of anyone's desire. I am sorry for saying mean things to just further your self-hate. I am sorry for all the time I made you feel bad about yourself.

I am telling you this because I can see that you are starting to change, and you are starting to see what everyone else sees. A beautiful, intelligent, hilarious, adventurous, brave, kind, generous, kick-ass woman! I love it when I hear you say these things out loud. I love it when you stand up for yourself and say no to things you do not want to do. I love how you started living your life the way you want to live. It has always been your life, and I love that you are finally a hawk. Yes, you are a hawk. You have your eyes focused on your goal. You soar in the sky staring at your goal, not taking your eyes away from it. You have your talons outstretched with precision, ready to take what is yours, ready to love every moment of your actions and your accomplishments.

Thank you for making this change, for believing in yourself and your own worth. I know that this journey is going to be amazing because it is finally your journey. It is going to be perfect because it is going to be just the way you want it. Go do something amazing, Dory, and remember, fuck what they think. This is your life, and that is the only explanation you need.

Love, me

PART 2

THAT DATING THING

So how do we start? How does a single person who has had their heart ripped out and used start over again? How do we make the past the past, live in the present, and create a future that we love?

I believe that is an answer that each of us needs to find on their own. What I have are my experiences and my dreams, so I will use those as ingredients in my recipe of finding true love.

Let me tell you about this year's Valentine's Day. First of all, in my opinion, this is the worst holiday for single people and, who are we kidding, for couples too! It is like this day of expectations and guaranteed disappointments. But hey, I love the sweet tart hearts, so at least there is good candy in the stores. Anyways, this year, I was sitting at home because it happens to be a Sunday. I was not doing much but watching a little TV, cleaning my house, playing with my dogs, and doing laundry. Meanwhile, my phone was collecting text after text from people wishing me a happy Valentine's Day.

First thing in the morning, I checked my phone, and there was a text from Ben. It read, "Dory I love you." Reading that made me feel so happy and devastated at the same time. We have been texting each other since he left, and they are mostly texts about how we both love each other, how our love was real, and he says that he is miserable and messed up his life when he left me. So, this text was really not that strange, but it hurt. I felt like a used sofa. He's hanging on to me and cannot let me go, but does not want me.

Second text I got was from Paul. He and I have been talking too because he has shared custody of his youngest son. My youngest and his youngest have stayed really close throughout the years. Now that his youngest lives with him part-time, I have contacted Paul to arrange overnights for the boys. From those, we started up a friend-ship, but nothing more. He has asked to date me again, but I have made it very clear that friendship is all I want. But I digress, Paul texted me that morning and said he still loves me and hopes that someday we will be together again and happy Valentine's Day.

Later in the day, I got a text from Sam, of course, him being the most mentally complicated person, and he sent me the most simple text. It read, "Happy Valentine's Day." That was it. I respond with a "You too," simple, just like Sam.

When I took my dogs for a walk, I got a much unexpected text from an unknown number. Apparently my sister gave my number to a guy she had met and thought he would be better suited for me. So this man, Ryan, texted me about getting my number from my sister and introduced himself. We texted back and forth for a bit, nothing serious, but we do have a lot in common, so I will probably pursue that one.

And finally, at about ten o'clock at night, I got an email from Carter, begging me for my phone number (apparently his wife deleted it from his phone and blocked my number). I thought about it, gave it to him, and immediately got a text from him saying after weeks of marriage counseling, his wife and he decided that a divorce was the right thing for them, and that they signed the paperwork and he is moving out in three weeks. He continued by saying that he loves me and wants me to be his girlfriend.

I felt like Clark Griswold, "Hallelujah, holy shit, where's the Tylenol." It is like they all got together in a huddle and said, "Hey, we were a bunch of assholes, and had no idea what we had when we had it so good with Dory [lots of grunting and high fives]! Let's really mess with her head this time and confess our love to her, but then do nothing about it and just make her feel loved and hurt all at the same time! *On four!* One to three, *break.*"

Yeah, kind of like that. I felt loved and then hurt because no one really wanted me. They just wanted me to want them so they could feel loved and keep me on a string so that they could have some thread of hope out there that I still loved them and would take them back at any second because I have nothing better to do! *Well, fuck that!*

Now Ryan, I needed to exclude him from this bunch of assholes because he did nothing wrong. But the rest of them, well, I needed to apply all of my lessons that I learned from them, forgive them, accept their faults, know my worth, and then say no, thank you.

I needed to clear my head. I needed to clear whatever thoughts I was putting out in the universe because apparently she is confused too! I needed to put my phone away. And that is exactly what I did. I decided that for a week, starting the day after Valentine's Day, I was taking a week off. I decided not to text nor respond to any texts from any of my exes. I was going to clear my mind and my phone. I would respond to only Ryan because he was the only one that I was interested in getting to know. I already know the others, and although I would love for Ben to come walking back into my house, swoop me up, kiss me all over, and tell me it was just a bad dream and that he loves me and wants to marry me, I know that is never going to happen. So, I had to move forward. And I was going to move forward with intention. In order to do that, I needed some silence and clarity.

I thought about sending out a group text and saying, "Hello, boys, each one of you has texted your love for me and regretted your decisions to not be with me, yet none of you were willing to put up the fight for me when it came down to it. So I am sorry, but I can no longer be your 'just in case' girl. So I am going to stop texting you, and I would appreciate if you would not text me either."

But I thought the group text, although undeniably hilarious for me, would not be the best way to go. So instead, I wrote to each one individually saying that I was hurting, I needed space to heal, and that their lack of commitment and current unhappiness is not my problem, so please, stop treating me like a desperate woman who is just pining for their love and give me the respect I deserve and not text me.

Honestly, it was extremely difficult because as you probably know by now, I have a hard time saying no. But since that was something I just recently learned, I knew that I just had to do it and that my action of saying no was the only way I was going to move on.

Carter was the first to respond. He said that he understood and that he loved me. Sam responded by saying he was proud of me for taking time for myself. Paul responded by also giving me support for my choice. Ben was silent.

The next day, I woke up with no text from anyone. It was strange, but also oddly nice. I did not have to think about anyone else's situation or feelings except for mine. I did not have to feel bad for anyone and their supposed horrible situation and expectation for my pity. I just went through my morning routine. Then around ten o'clock, I got a refreshing text from Ryan, the new guy. I was happy to hear from him, and since I have no history with him, there were no expectations. We texted back and forth for a while, and then we both had other things to do. Later that afternoon, I took my dogs on a walk. These walks are my time to free my mind and process. I was thinking about how much energy it takes for me to tend to all of these men's feelings. I felt like I had so much more energy to commit to myself and toward procuring a new, healthy relationship. I started to feel better, almost like the fog was lifting, and the sun was just starting to peek through. Do I dare say it, I felt happy.

That feeling lasted for a while, and Ryan and I texted a bit more that afternoon. Other than that, my phone was silent.

Maybe I have finally done it? Maybe I finally gave them the information they needed to leave me alone. I actually stood up for myself instead of feeling sorry for them. I did what I needed. So far it feels great.

> You read about love in a book somewhere
> Then you read it out loud what you found in there
> And you had me for days and you had me for months
> And I hope you've enjoyed your time of fun
> Oh, forgive me
> For running down your door
> I thought all those fancy words were yours
> I'm treated with cold, cold kisses
> And I'm treasured like a piece of junk
> I call you up to say I love you

You only call me when you're drunk
And still you keep me hanging around
Like I was some old sofa you found in a second-
hand store ("Forgive Me," Ida Marie)

TO BE PICKY OR
TO NOT BE PICKY

During the time that I had silenced my exes, Ryan and I started to get to know each other more, of course, just through text and phone calls. We sent a few pictures here and there, and then slowly things started to get a bit sexier. We talked about meeting up (he lives about four hours away from me) halfway and going for a hike. But then, as most conversations with men go, he started texting sexual desires. He was very polite about it, asked my permission before he talked about it, and also said that he respected any boundaries that I had. It turned out to be a bit erotic, but also romantic. I kept it light because I am just not that vocal over text. I would much rather be in person. Plus, I have not even met this person, so who knows if I would even be attracted to him.

So here is my dilemma, when you are a forty-three-year-old single mother of two teenage kids, how do you date, how do you not waste your time, yet not be too picky?

Is being picky a good thing? Or will it limit my dating pool so much that I will be alone forever?

I think that I should have been pickier in my past. I know that if I had stuck to my nonnegotiables about what I want in a partner that I would not have dated Ben nor Paul. But is that necessarily a good thing? Look at all the amazing experiences I had with them and the lessons I learned.

The hardest part for me is if I am not picky or intentional in what I want in a partner, then I am going to end up in a situation once again where I have to tell them no, thank you. So would I rather be honest with myself and my partner up front or have to do it later and possibly hurt myself and them? I am trying to change the way I do things, so I am going to try and be honest up front.

So what do I need to be picky about? What are my nonnegotiables? I think this is a really great question and something that all of us should reflect upon. Even if we are in a relationship that is either going well or getting rough. If we look at our nonnegotiables and make a list, then we can really be specific and not necessarily picky. Some online dating websites are really good at this. Before you even make your profile, they ask you question after question about how you feel about certain "important" issues in a relationship. These can include religion, physical looks, fitness, politics, hobbies, careers, etc. But I want to go beyond that. So, I am going to really dive into the details and make a list of my no-negotiables.

Here is my list. Feel free to steal this and add or change it!

My future partner must be the following:

- Must be tolerant and kind to all people regardless of religion, gender, race, etc.
- Must love animals and children
- Must have a career/job/income
- Must love the outdoors
- Must not live with parents
- Must have a vehicle
- Must have health insurance
- Must be hilarious
- Must not be an angry person
- Must be intelligent
- Must not be intimidated by strong/brave/independent women
- Must be able to express love
- Must be affectionate
- Must be a great lover
- Must love traveling
- Must have an education
- Must not be lazy

- Must be as tall or taller than me
- Must be attractive to me
- Must be attracted to me
- Must be proud of me and want to introduce me to friends and family

Is that too many? Hell no! I think I may even have more, but as of right now, those are my nonnegotiables. I added in health insurance because I do not want to be financially responsible for my partner's health issues. I would include a good credit score because I think that is extremely sexy, but I am willing for that to be a preference, not a nonnegotiable. How is this list going to help or possibly hinder my prospective love life?

I think that it is only going to help me because the more specific I am, the more likely I am to have a lasting, healthy relationship. I also think that there are going to be a lot of guys out there that actually meet this list and go beyond my expectations. The likelihood of that is very high, and I know this because it actually just happened.

It's been about six months since my last haircut. I needed a trim, so I called my stylist. He is amazing, so good-looking, talented, funny, and I have been going to him for fourteen years, so it is easy to talk to him. I called and left a message but no response, so I called and left a message again. Still no response. By that time, I started wondering (1) if he is okay or (2) if he does just not want me as a client anymore. Either way, I desperately needed a haircut, so maybe this was just the universe telling me to go somewhere else. So that is what I did. I called up a new place and made an appointment.

The day of my haircut, my regular stylist finally called, left me a message telling me that he had been out of town. Well, that sucks, but too late. As I was walking to the salon, I started saying in my head, "Okay, I am really ready to meet someone new. I am sick of missing my ex, and I want to move on. Spring is coming, and it will be a great time to meet a guy because we can be outside in nature." I think, hmmmm, maybe the reason I had to book this new appointment is because I am going to meet the man of my dreams in this new salon.

I entered the salon, got to the waiting area, and soon walked in a man calling his next client's name, Dory. I looked up, and there stood a nice and tall man. Really skinny, but handsome. He introduced himself and then took me back to sit in the styling chair to talk about my desired cut. We got through the discussion, headed back to the shampooing station, and there we started talking. We talked through the entire haircut. This is what I found out. This guy is friendly and funny, his parents live on a property near my parents, and he helps them out on the farm. He loves raising animals and has two adorable dogs. He went to school here and moved away to attend a trade school. He has an education and has traveled a lot. He loves camping and working hard on his parents' farm. He wants to build a house on their property to help raise the cattle. He loves his family and is very close to his parents and siblings. He is single. Do you see what is happening here? He is hitting everything on my list. But wait, there's more. He just sold his old beat-up 2003 Subaru and bought a 2006 Toyota Tacoma. When we realized how this was almost the exact same case with me, he asked me, "What color is yours?" I said, "White," and guess what? Yep! So is his! Coincidence? I think not!

I walked out of the salon, with a great haircut, and thought, what the hell was that, universe? Were you just trying to prove a point? Well, if you were, then you succeeded! I get it, there are going to be a lot of men out there that are available and that pass my list, so my question about being too picky, well, that is no longer a question of mine. I was not very attracted to the stylist and he looked pretty young, so it was not like I wanted to pursue anything. It was more about the experience of it all and getting whipped with the "stop worrying so much" stick by the universe.

I have decided that I am going to be specific, not picky. I am going to make sure that I do not date anyone that does not pass my nonnegotiables, but I am going to be flexible about other things because I may find something attractive or intriguing that I otherwise would have thought otherwise. So specific and not picky.

Well, folks, there you have it. You now have read through my journey of love, loss, redemption, falling, and now dating. I know this new adventure is going to be amazing, and I know that change is happening. I am now a soaring hawk, taking this life by my talons and being grateful for the depths of the canyon below and lessons of forgiveness, acceptance, self-worth, and, ultimately, self-love.

Love, me.

About the Author

Dory Daniel currently resides in Durango, Colorado with her two teenage boys, fourteen chickens, three ducks, two cats, and two dogs. She has been a schoolteacher for over twelve years and has a passion for the Spanish language and travel. Dory is an active adventure seeker and loves spending her summers being a raft guide on the Animas River, as well as hiking and camping throughout Colorado and Utah.

CPSIA information can be obtained
at www.ICGtesting.com
Printed in the USA
BVHW032337211221
624508BV00022B/248

9 781662 452956